Learning for Sustainability

Learning for Sustainability

Peter Senge Joe Laur Sara Schley Bryan Smith

society for SoL
organizational learning

CAMBRIDGE, MASSACHUSETTS

Published by SoL (The Society for Organizational Learning, Inc.)

25 First Street, Suite 414

Cambridge, MA 02141 USA

1-617-300-9500

publisher@solonline.org

SoL is a nonprofit global membership organization whose purpose is to discover, integrate, and implement theories and practices for the interdependent development of people and their institutions. A portion of the net proceeds from SoL publishing sales are reinvested in basic research, leading-edge applied learning projects, and building a global network of learning communites. For information on membership, professional development opportunities, events, and other publications—including the e-journal *Reflections*—please visit www.solonline.org.

Editor: Ann Graham

Book design: Chris Welch

Library of Congress Control Number: 2006924486

ISBN 10: 0-9742390-2-X

ISBN 13: 978-0-9742390-2-6

Contents

1

The Fifth Discipline Meets Sustainability

Peter Senge, Joe Lauer, Sara Schley, Bryan Smith

Throughout the world today, people from all walks of life feel uneasy. Despite dazzling technology advances and improved material standards of living for many, the gap between "haves" and "have-nots" is growing, and people sense unprecedented dangers from environmental imbalances that could provoke disaster—even making the planet uninhabitable for humans and other species. At the same time, humanity has the potential to effect a postindustrial renaissance of unimaginable beauty and value. It is the best and worst of futures that face us.

Over the last 20 years, as people around the world have become more aware of the persistent threats to, and dysfunctions in, modern lifestyles, the word sustainability has come into use in discussions of healthier, more positive ways of living. The broad definition of sustainability coined in the book *Our Common Future*, published by the United Nations' World Commission on Environment and Development in 1987, introduced the business world to a new goal for economic development: To "meet the needs of the present generation without compromising the ability of future generations to meet their own needs."[1] (See the Sustainability Lexicon on page 44.)

For the business community, particularly for multinational corporations, the U.N. report established sustainability as a code word for a variety of emerging standards and expectations by which society judges the performance of corporations, and by which corporations can judge themselves. Since then, the concept of sustainability has broadened. It is now an umbrella term for all of the aims and norms that encourage corporations, organizations, and society at large to more effectively address the adverse social and environmental effects of commerce and the dangers of narrowly pursuing maximization of profits regardless of the larger costs.

The sustainability agenda is inherently ambiguous because it incorporates two distinct aspirations: reducing unsustainability (by improving practices that are dangerous and wasteful) and creating generative sustainability (innovating toward a world that ensures human and natural systems can flourish together).[2] For the most part, the first aim dominates the present political debates and business strategies: reducing emissions, improving eco-efficiency, giving aid to nations left behind by globalization. But as William McDonough and Michael Braungart write in their book, *Cradle to Cradle*, being "less bad" does not make one good, and it is questionable whether our present problems can be solved by approaches that, by and large, preserve business as usual.[3] There is a crucial need today for compelling images of a future we truly want to create: an economic system that operates in accord with natural principles and generates no waste, an energy system powered entirely by net energy from the sun, and an ethic of being common villagers who must all live together on an increasingly interdependent planet. Articulating such images is not enough; we must develop the confidence that we can actually advance in this direction. For business leaders, this means moving from a compliance mentality of doing no harm to the aggressive creation of products, processes, business models, and companies that are truly creating restorative and enduring wealth—leaving communities and larger living systems in better condition, not worse.

While not denying the extraordinary difficulties and complexity of the challenges we all face, we want to emphasize one optimistic message: Using our creative capacity in collaboration with others, we can create a world we will be proud to leave our grandchildren. The capability is ours, if we choose to develop and exercise it, and many people and organizations are already doing just that.

This small book, published by the Society for Organizational Learning, has been written as a vehicle for sparking conversation and encouraging dialogue about how to develop this confidence and these capabilities. We emphasize the role of businesses and other organizations in both reducing unsustainability and creating sustainability because we believe they hold a particular key to the future. And given the need for bold leadership and deep learning by institutions and individuals, we are especially interested in connecting the "inner" and "outer" work that must be done: This includes connecting the inner changes in how we manage and lead with the outer effects our organizations have on larger systems; connecting the inner changes in mental models and personal visions with the outer changes in management culture; and connecting the inner changes in who we are as human beings with how we act and interact.

This book is also based on our appreciation for how organizations amplify human power. As Peter Drucker says, the purpose of an organization or enterprise is to enable ordinary people to do extraordinary things. The stories, essays, and exercises we share here show, in particular, people inside organizations who are wrestling with the challenges of defining what sustainability means for their organization, and working to make sustainability principles and perspectives a part of mainstream business practice. We want to help readers articulate what sustainability means in their context, convey the relationship between sustainability and business success, and express the value for everyone of operating in closer harmony with natural systems and human systems.

Many important books have laid out in great detail the negative consequences of the last 150 years of industrial development. Our job is to tell the positive stories of people who have heard those messages, and are doing something about it. This book is intended as a guide for leaders at all levels engaged in all types of enterprises, local and global.

We must work together to create living organizations in tune with the social and natural world. The word inspire means to "breathe life into." Our aim is to inspire change agents: people who know that sustainability matters, but who also know we all have a lot to learn about what it means, and who understand the hard work it will take to achieve the necessary changes.

We believe fervently that if the world is to move past its current danger point into a new postindustrial renaissance, systems thinking and other learning disciplines are crucial. This involves not just the specific tools of systems thinking, dialogue, working with mental models, personal mastery, and building shared visions, but the broader set of attitudes, values, and practices embodied in each one of them. Inspired by the work of SoL's Sustainability Consortium, a learning community of diverse companies (large multinational and midsized regional firms from multiple industries) instigated by coauthors Joe Laur and Sara Schley, the articles here examine how individuals and organizations can build their capabilities in areas critical to the work of sustainability, such as gaining shared understanding of complex systems, developing deeper listening and dialogue skills, growing trusting relationships and action networks, and forming and nurturing multi-institutional partnerships.

It is a core theory of systems thinking that new ideas, connections, and social networks underlie all large-scale systemic change. This contrasts with the theory that change occurs through some centralized force of power. Daniel Quinn said the first Industrial Revolution was not a "utopian undertaking," but the product of a million small beginnings that didn't proceed according to some theoretical design.[4]

A new era in human development is not going to arise because governments decree it, or because a few companies change their strategies. It will happen because a diffuse and diverse critical mass of people and organizations decide to live and act differently—as parents, as professionals and as leaders, as suppliers and as customers, as citizens and as entrepreneurs, as friends and as colleagues, as teachers and as students.

2

Creating Positive Futures in an Interdependent World

Peter Senge

At the World Economic Forum in January 2005, British Prime Minister Tony Blair declared interdependence to be:

> the governing characteristic of modern international politics.
> . . . We may disagree about the nature of the problems and how
> to resolve them, but no nation, however powerful, seriously
> believes today that these problems can be resolved alone.
> Interdependence is no longer disputed.

Indeed, there has never before been a time when the social, economic, and ecological conditions that challenge political leaders in any one part of the world have been so interwoven with what is occurring in so many other places. This phenomenon has arisen through the ever-growing web of interconnectedness spun by institutions, especially multinational corporations. Our actions as individuals—intentional or inadvertent—are mediated and magnified as they play out through this global web. Collectively, these organizations determine what technologies are created and how they are applied around the world; which markets develop and which ones are largely ignored. These institutions determine who benefits from the global economy and who does not.

And they are responsible for almost inconceivable phenomena—the shifting of the chemical balance in the atmosphere—even within our own bodies—and the altering of cultures that, before such interventions, were unchanged for centuries.

On the one hand, the global industrial system promoting instant communication, individual autonomy, and consumption has the potential to make life on earth materially better for more people than ever before. At the same time, we also see titanic institutional forces threatening the health of ecosystems and social systems in ways that could permanently degrade the quality of life on earth for all living beings.

The Alien Future

What does it mean for us, individually and together, to be part of this web of interdependence? Consider the terrorist attacks of September 11, 2001. Was this event political, religious, environmental, cultural, or economic? I believe it was all of these, as well as a powerful reminder to a quite insular society, the United States, that it is not an island that can pursue its own way of doing things and expect to be left alone. Terrorism is something that Europeans have lived with for a long time. The idea that it could happen to citizens of the United States was shocking. In the actions of one morning, a handful of people virtually crippled the U.S. economy for a significant period of time. That's interdependence.

However, the costs of interdependence, and our vulnerability to it, are with us every day; September 11 was simply a highly visible and drastic example. Trend Micro, an American information security firm, shows the cost of computer virus damage to American companies jumping from $13 billion in 2001, to approximately $25 billion in 2002, to $55 billion in 2003. In business, such "cyberterrorism" is stunning, but is also an accepted fact of life for CIOs and others responsible for maintaining global information infrastructures.[5] Or consider the resources wasted in a global food system in which countries simultaneously import and export hundreds of thousands of tons of the same commodity foods. The average pound of food on an American's dinner plate travels 2,000 miles before it makes its way to the table. It is hard to fathom that governments and companies perpetuate such a needless transport burden when we live in a world struggling to lessen human impacts on the environment.[6]

Because the daily costs of interdependence are difficult to see, leaders like Mr. Blair face the dilemma of either seeming to "cry wolf" when there is no obvious threat, or reacting aggressively to threats, such as global warming, that have political currency but are far removed from the underlying and systemic causes of problems.

To be sure, throughout history a few human beings—philosophers, spiritual teachers, and writers—have recognized the effects of human interdependence, pondering both the difficulties and benefits it poses. Speaking about the liberation of the human spirit, American writer Maya Angelou tells of an African playwright, Terence, a former slave living in Rome around 150 B.C. who said, "I am a human being. Nothing human can be alien to me." In this simple declaration, Terence established a profound personal connection to all of human behavior—from the most admired behaviors to the most heinous. For Maya Angelou, this awakening to our universality catalyzes the capacity for compassion among human beings, a prerequisite for all of us living together in healthier ways. Similarly, societies, and their representative institutions, stepping consciously into their place within the global web, must recognize their kinship and interdependence. Societies must also learn how to move beyond blame and separation when there is trouble.

The problem is that human beings usually don't think this way. We have been conditioned for thousands of years to identify with the ways in which we are separate—as members of families, tribes, religions; as citizens of villages, countries, and nation-states—but not with the one thing we have in common: We are all human, and we are all together on one planet. Organizations are conditioned to have the same self-interested focus. As a result, few are prepared to serve a truly global society. And why should we expect them to be? There is simply no precedent for individuals, institutions, or societies to face their global citizenship.

The immensity of this challenge was beautifully articulated by Mieko Nishimizu, then a vice president of the World Bank for Southeast Asia. During her tenure, Nishimizu was involved in pioneering efforts involving energy, water, and the development of indicators of sustainable national development, such as Bhutan's Gross National Happiness Index. (In 1999 the Planning Commission of Bhutan published Bhutan 2020, a government vision statement that declared "the key to happiness is to be found, once basic material needs have been met, in the satisfaction of non-material needs and in emotional and spiritual growth.")[7]

Speaking in September 2002 to an audience of world leaders on the occasion of the 50th anniversary of Japan's entering the post-World War II Bretton Woods Agreements, Nishimizu, who grew up in a middle-class home in Japan, began by sharing her personal journey of coming to terms with poverty. She described walking with a woman from Bangladesh for two hours, each way, to get her daily water. As they walked, the woman told Nishimizu, "This is not living. This is keeping a body alive." Nishimizu knew that the conditions in which this woman lived—a reality for increasing numbers of people in drought-stricken areas around the world—could not be separated from the forces of global interdependence. Many in the north of the Indian subcontinent today suffer the consequences of drying rivers and chronic dehydration, in part, because of reduced spring glacier melts in the Himalayas. The glaciers there, as almost everywhere else in the world, are contracting due to global warming.

In her speech, Nishimizu summarized the effects of our growing interdependence with the haunting phrase: "The future appears alien to us."

She continued:

It differs from the past most notably in that the earth itself is the relevant unit from which to frame and measure the future. Discriminating issues that shape the future are all fundamentally global. We belong to one inescapable network of mutuality. Mutuality of ecosystems, mutuality of freer movement of information, ideas, people, capital, goods and services, and mutuality of peace and security. We are tied, indeed, in a single fabric of destiny on Planet Earth. Policies and actions that attempt to tear a nation from this cloth will inevitably fail by impoverishing the very wealth or income of those they set out to protect.

Learning to See Through the Alienness

Interdependence is not a new problem for humankind. Throughout history, there have been imbalances created by interdependencies we do not see, many of them eventually self-correcting. The Middle East was once the Fertile Crescent, before it was deforested into desert by thousands of years of agricultural expansion that went beyond natural limits. Since the beginning of industrialization, however, the human capacity to generate imbalances in the local and especially the global natural environment has expanded dramatically. Increasing carbon dioxide (CO_2) in the atmosphere is one of several accumulating effects; for many experts, it is the most worrisome.

Although we have not been able to achieve a global consensus on the actions that need to be taken to reduce greenhouse gas emissions, there is less and less disagreement about the basic conclusion that continued accumulation of CO_2 in the atmosphere threatens both global temperature averages and weather stability.

The former effect can be seen clearly in the following charts published by the United Nations Framework Convention on Climate Change (UNFCCC). Chart 1 shows the earth's average surface temperature since the mid-1800s. On average, current day temperatures are almost one degree Celsius higher than they were 140 years ago.

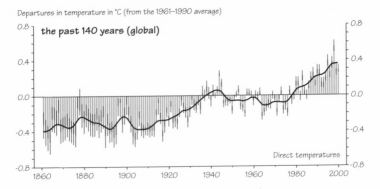

Departures in temperature in °C (from the 1961–1990 average)

the past 140 years (global)

Direct temperatures

The next UNFCCC chart shows that the amount of CO_2 (in millions of tons) released by industry and motor vehicles has risen steadily since 1971, with an accelerating rate of increase from the Asia-Pacific region and continued increases from industrialized countries. The United States alone now produces almost 30 percent of global CO_2 emissions.

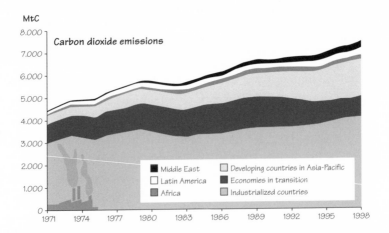

MtC

Carbon dioxide emissions

■ Middle East   □ Developing countries in Asia-Pacific
□ Latin America   ■ Economies in transition
■ Africa   ☐ Industrialized countries

To be sure, the increase in temperature of one degree Celsius might not have been much to worry about—assuming it stopped there. In fact, many argue that such an increase might well have been generated by natural oscillations having nothing to do with carbon emissions. But the next chart, showing long-term oscillations in atmospheric gases over the past 400,000 years (based on analysis of ice core samples from Antarctica) dispels this view. From this data, it is apparent that the current level of CO_2 is already 30 percent higher than at any time during this historical period, which covers four major ice ages and the intervening warming periods, including the past 10,000 years or so, during which human population and activity has spread dramatically. The chart below shows today's average annual temperature (T) to be slightly below prior historical peaks.

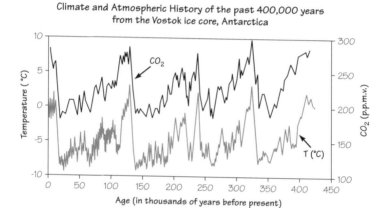

Climate and Atmospheric History of the past 400,000 years
from the Vostok ice core, Antarctica

So what can be said about the future? Much is uncertain. But applying a few basic systems thinking tools goes a long way toward making sense of our predicament. First, given the delays built into the atmospheric system, even if CO_2 levels stopped rising today, temperatures would likely continue to rise for many years—just as the temperature rises for a period of time after you roll up the windows of a car parked in the sunshine. Even more telling is the current gap between emissions and the rate at which CO_2 is being taken out of the atmosphere today. Think of the present concentration of CO_2 in the atmosphere as the level of a bathtub, with emissions as the "inflow" and carbon sequestration by green plants in the sea and on the surface of the Earth as the "outflow." Although the precise rate of global carbon sequestration is not known, the scientific consensus is that it less than one-half the inflow.[8] That is, carbon dioxide is filling up the atmosphere about twice as quickly as it is "draining out." This means that, if every country in the world (including the United States and China, the world's second largest CO_2 emitter) signed and followed the current Kyoto Protocol, which calls for leveling CO_2 emissions at 1990 levels, CO_2 would still grow in the atmosphere forever. Stabilizing CO_2 would take more than a 50 percent reduction in emissions worldwide. No one knows how such a shift in industrial activity might occur. It is safe to say, though, that without such a change, far more severe effects of CO_2 buildup will be felt in the coming decades.

Restoring Human Wisdom

The challenges we face can seem overwhelming. In fact, they are overwhelming us because we don't appreciate the exquisite web of interconnectedness that enables life in the universe. Wherever we stand, we stand within a web. Human wisdom expressed in many deep-rooted and varied societal traditions around the world has long acknowledged that an understanding of systems in their totality is the only foundation for making sound choices that benefit the health of the whole.

I believe humans have innate capacities, beyond social conditioning, to develop a holistic awareness of their relationship with the world. Activating these capacities starts with seeing the connection between human consciousness and the physical world. This foundational concept is now reentering the mainstream of Western culture. Diverse new scientific theories are legitimating this ancient idea, ranging from the esoteric frontiers of quantum theory (where it is now widely accepted that measured quantum states do not exist independent of how we try to measure them) to systems theory, which continually reminds us that our perceptions of reality shape our actions and, consequently, that reality.

To impact society, this new understanding must penetrate business, education, government, and other core institutions. The professionals in these institutions must create more inclusive and integrated ways of living and working. Such change must encompass diverse global movements, whether holistic health, restorative justice, or learner-centered learning in schools. In business, it will mean recognizing, as interdependence grows, that there are more effective alternatives than managing with traditional hierarchical power. More and more businesses are striving for fewer layers of management and more "self-organization." More and more are breaking free of mechanical notions of top-down control, starting to see organizations as living systems rather than, as Arie de Geus, author of *The Living Company* has said, machines for producing money. Again, older notions of self-organizing and self-governing exist throughout the world, in many native and indigenous cultures—wherever human beings have tried to understand nature deeply and to live in accord with its teachings.

When I have heard executives in global companies talk candidly about the future, their real concern usually is not the cost of capital or return on sales; it is the social and political stability of the world they will leave behind. They, too, see the future as an alien place. If it is to become more hospitable, we must rediscover and more effectively apply the human wisdom that is in *our* nature.

A Journey in Time

Joe Laur and Sara Schley

Where is your greatest personal leverage for moving toward a vision of sustainability—your opportunity to make the greatest impact with the least effort? What are the mental models—the attitudes and implicit theories about the way the world works—that shape your perception and guide your actions? Which of these mental models are linked to your most effective actions now, and which were inherited from your family? Which might we need to adapt to create the world we want to leave to our great-grandchildren?

In this exercise, you will seek answers to these questions by stepping back from day-to-day pressures to see your life in its broad historical context. This exercise is as close as most people get to imagining their own story at the heart of "seven generations": three or more in the past, and three or more in the future.

1. Ancestors: In your mind, go back in time 100 years. At the time of the publication of this book, that would be the year 1906. Picture the world of your great- or great-great-grandparents.

Where did they live? Did they live in the same country where you live now, or had they migrated there from elsewhere? What kind of home did they have, as far as you know? What was their livelihood?

What technologies were they accustomed to? What kinds of nature? How do you know?

Consider everything you have heard (through the stories told in your family) or read (through their letters and journals, or through clippings passed to you) about the world, society, and commerce of that time. What were the paradigms, mind-sets, and mental models that shaped the attitudes and values that your great-great-grandparents or great-grandparents held? How did those attitudes and values then pass on through successive generations, down to you? If you do not know anything about previous generations, what do you imagine they felt, saw, and thought?

In a workshop where we conducted this exercise, one participant talked about her great-grandparents, who migrated from farms in Poland to New York, riding in steerage in the early 1900s. They settled in the Bronx, then a great burgeoning sub-city in America, and sent for each of their brothers and sisters in Poland, one by one. They never lost their sense of joy about their new home, but they also were fiercely protective, expecting every stranger to be an enemy, afraid that anything they had might be stolen at any moment. "They would never understand," she said, "the simple trust I have to have in people I meet at work, simply to get things done."

Another individual said that there was an ethic of thrift in their family due to economic hardships in Ireland that transformed into energy conservation practices today. Yet another, who grew up in a wealthy Latin American family, explained that the notion of a land of endless forests, rivers, oceans, and opportunities had led to a wasteful, throwaway mind-set in his family (and in some of his most deeply held attitudes).

2. From the past to now: What coaching might your great-grandparents have for you today? Which mental models shaped today's world to their liking, and which have had unintended side effects that they would want you to mitigate?

One workshop participant imagined his grandparents saying: "Everything we threw into the woods in northern Minnesota really did go away, decaying or rusting into the ground beneath our 'dump.' We thought nature would take care of it all somehow. But now, the plastics and chemicals that you throw away come back to haunt you. We wish we had left you a different way of handling garbage."

3. Descendants in the best possible world: Now go forward in time 100 years. If you have children, it is the time of your great-grandchildren or great-great-grandchildren. It is the world of future generations. What is the best possible future you can imagine for these people, your literal or figurative heirs? How might their mental models and world views differ from those you hold today?

One individual answered this question by saying: "It is very clear that two major things are different. People live decades longer than they did 100 years ago; and they live close together, in beautiful, green cities, traveling from one to another without making any more waste than water."

Another said: "It's really the case, in this world 100 years from now, that any girl can grow up to be president."

And a third imagined her great-granddaughter returning to tell her, "Waste equals food. We live that way now. Indeed, we've adopted the basic principles of living things: Protect the young above all else, live only on what the sun produces, treat all waste as food for someone or something else. And diversity beats homogeneity every time."

4. From the best possible future to now: Stand in that future. Imagine the people who live there (this may include you, if you imagine yourself living that long). From that imagined time, look back to yourself as you are today. What would the people who live then say to you in the present, about the ways and means of making these far-flung aspirations real?

"Take risks," guessed one participant. "Learn from your mistakes, think about our world and what we will inherit, start where you are and take each day as it comes."

5. Evolving toward your aspiration: Imagine yourself only 10 years in the future: a decade older than you are today. What is the best possible world you can envision for that time? What is your life like? What are you doing? What has meaning and vitality for you?

Presumably, this world of 10 years hence will represent an evolution toward the best possible future that you envisioned for the next century in Step 3. How will the conditions 10 years from now shape the world of 100 years from now?

Stand in that place, 10 years from now. How would you coach yourself today, in the present, about how to build toward that future you envisioned 10 years away?

An engineer at a major electronics firm saw that his love of technology could be used to create more sustainable products and services.

An automotive designer saw herself working not just on vehicles powered by internal combustion engines, but on a variety of new kinds of vehicles.

The CEO of a textile chemicals firm began to wonder what it would mean for the firm to not merely reduce pollution, but generate improvement in the natural environment around its facilities.

6. The path: See yourself one year in the future, on the road to that world to which you aspire. How are you living your life? What is your life like? What are you doing? What has meaning and vitality for you? How are you building a path toward the world you envisioned 10 years and 100 years hence?

The engineer saw that he could develop a program that would let him work half of his job in sustainability areas—bringing e-commerce to the poorest of the poor and including poor nations in the Internet world. Later, he asked for, and got, the job assignment.

The designer saw that she could make a move back to her native country and work there on sustainable mobility issues in partnership with an NGO. She too later asked for, and won, the assignment.

The CEO of the textile chemicals firm saw that by moving three engineers from the end of the development cycle to the front, he could prevent the waste and pollution they were currently working to remediate.

7. Current reality: Return to the present moment. Think about the commitments that would be needed to reach those points in the future—100 years, 10 years, and one year from now. What would have to happen in service of those goals to achieve them? What might they be calling you, and others, to do differently?

The CEO said: "I know now that I must always think upstream, to the beginning of every process, to the design, development, and very reason for the product in the first place. That's where the trouble is designed in—or out."

More specifically, where do you want to be one year from now? What would have to change, starting now, to allow you to get there in time?

A manager at a motorcycle firm noted that just changing the way he thought about these issues on a day-to-day basis made a difference. He resolved to tape a picture of the earth from space above his desk, along with his children's pictures, to remind him to take them both into account when making decisions.

8. Stepping back: Suppose you had conducted this exercise 10 years ago—or one year ago. What might you have seen? What might you have changed, in your practices or personal life? If you had made those changes, what might be different today?

One engineer said, "I turned down a chance for training in team leadership a few years ago. I now see that a lot of my new role is going to involve raising questions with others whom I don't directly supervise, and I'm going to need some help. Some kind of training would have made a difference."

9. Commitment: An exercise like this always leads to a moment of choice. Without choice, there is no commitment. So: With all the authenticity and self-awareness you can muster, what choices are you willing to make right now? To what changes do you commit? What thoughts and attitudes are you ready to shift?

10. Reflection: Take a few minutes to jot down some of the insights that you gained from this journey through time. Given the opportunity, what might you have said to your ancestors 100 years ago? What is the potential future saying to you now? Where are your energy and capability strongest, and how can they help you take constructive action in moving toward your aspirations?

4

Engaging the Future

Bryan Smith

I magine you are the CFO of a major U.S. electric utility that is rapidly expanding into a global company, with important investments in developing countries. You are attending an executive team meeting early Monday morning. During a relatively routine discussion on an agenda item about next year's capital budget for the company's coal-, oil-, and gas-fired generating facilities, this heated skirmish occurs:

TED (VP, ENVIRONMENTAL HEALTH AND SAFETY): Global oil and gas production is going to peak and begin to decline within the next five years. This will cause major disruptions in supply and rapidly escalating prices for oil, gas, coal, uranium, and all other conventional fuels. To prepare for this, we need to swing at least 30 percent of our future capital allocations to renewables beginning next year.

JOANNE (VP, OPERATIONS): Breakthroughs in technologies for oil and gas exploration will lead to discovery of huge new reserves. Oil and gas prices will definitely stabilize or decline and we . . .

STAN (VP, PUBLIC AFFAIRS) (interrupting Joanne): But even with ample supplies of coal, oil, and gas, we may still get clobbered by carbon taxes in many of our markets. Public pressure for action on climate change is growing exponentially around the world. And pollution from coal-fired power plants in China is causing riots and widespread social unrest. As these incidents and harsh government actions to crush them get wide publicity globally, it will trigger similar unrest and challenges elsewhere.

ROBERT (CEO): I don't believe the science on climate change is strong enough for us to change our strategy. This is a temporary issue that will fade quickly when it dawns on people that it will cost them their jobs. I have seen issues like this come and go many times in my career here. And I agree with Joanne—there is no way we are going to run out of oil and gas in our lifetimes. It is a waste of time to worry about that.

ANTHONY (VP, STRATEGY): Robert, you have every right to your opinions about climate change and oil and gas reserves, but what are the implications for the future of our company if you are wrong on both issues?

As you listen to this conversation in your role as CFO, you conclude that Anthony's question to the CEO is the most crucial portion of this exchange. You had the same gnawing question in the back of your mind before Anthony spoke. But the next question on your mind is "How can I intervene effectively here so that our whole team can surface and address this uneasiness that many of us feel? I know that several other members of the team have voiced similar fears outside our meetings, but there is no forum to raise them together."

Rest assured that there are good answers to that question, but your first step is to stand in the shoes of Robert as CEO and understand his point of view, assumptions, and mental models. Robert instinctively feels fully justified in forcefully advocating that he has the best plan. After all, he has had an exemplary 30-year career with the company, and, during the last 10 years as CEO, has led one of the most successful periods in the 80-year history of the company—primarily by maintaining a steady course when others overreacted. He has been successful in the past by insisting that the company focus on one best prediction of the future and ignore the noise of other variables and forces that distract people from driving the business forward for growth.

Robert's predictions over time, including his views today, are consistent with his personal beliefs and mental models, and represent a continuation of the past 20 years or more of his experience in key leadership roles in the company, focused primarily on the U.S. market. His world view is made up of variables with which he is familiar and comfortable. He has high confidence in his ability to control his company's future the way he has controlled the company up to now. But is that confidence well founded?

On the surface, his views are convincing and seem to represent the lowest-risk strategy, but a wider view of emerging global forces suggests Robert's strategy may carry higher risk than he realizes. And that risk emanates from the way he and some of his executive team think about the future. Their way of employing their historic mental models to provide a feeling of comfort and confidence about the future is typical. But it may be masking deeper uncertainties that need to be brought to the surface, whether they are uncomfortable to consider or not.

The Risks of Predictions

Since the shock of the energy crisis in the early 1970s, the risks and opportunity costs of building any company's strategies around a single preferred picture of the future have been quietly but steadily increasing. And between 1970 and 1990, Royal Dutch/Shell moved from the bottom of the pack of global oil companies (known then as the Seven Sisters) to near the top.

This success is often credited to the resilient strategies provoked by the multiple future scenarios Royal Dutch/Shell executives created, including some that seemed very unlikely to occur, like the first energy crisis. But the real key to their success was in how the executive teams in Shell operating companies around the world actively used these seemingly improbable stories about the future to challenge their mental models and drive the creation of options. For example, many executives from other oil companies knew that the energy crisis could happen, but tended to discount that possibility in relation to their preferred prediction—relatively stable oil prices, in keeping with past trends.

Only Shell's executives spent a significant amount of time thinking through their strategies in light of the possibility of such a crisis occurring. Even though it wasn't certain, it triggered their creativity; they pioneered the use of flexible refining processes that could handle any type of crude oil available, they developed trading practices that allowed them to allocate oil supplies where they would be most needed, and for many years they decentralized management control so that regional managers could adapt to differing country responses to supply shortfalls and price instability. These practices would probably have served Shell well even if the oil supply crisis hadn't taken place; they turned out to be crucial forms of leverage when the crisis did occur.

Now fast-forward to 2001. Prior to September 11, few people suspected that successful terrorist attacks on the United States, using airplanes to destroy key buildings, were even possible, let alone likely. Yet in a scenario called "Fortress World" (one of a set of three scenarios developed in 1995-96 and published in the book *Which World* by Allen Hammond in 1998), shocking events like the terrorist attacks of September 11 were portrayed as a highly plausible outcome of widening gaps between haves and have-nots, and of hordes of desperate, unemployed young people joining a rapidly rising number of idealistic and nihilistic terrorist organizations. Leaders in charge of counterintelligence efforts proposed strategies and tactics to counter those organizations, but they didn't gain enough of a voice to be influential. They might have been far more persuasive if they had been able to actively explore these scenarios and their implications with key decision makers, instead of simply advocating their point of view.

Like preparation for terrorist attacks before 2001, sustainability is rarely incorporated into the heart of most companies' business strategies. Why does this integration occur so rarely? Clues can be found in the executive team conversation above. Both Ted (VP, Environmental Health & Safety?) and Stan (VP, Public Affairs) set the course of the conversation by advocating for a specific sustainability issue (peak oil production), and attempted to convince the others to place a big financial bet based on that one prediction, taking immediate action.

Joanne and Robert had very different predictions about the future, defined sustainability issues as nonstrategic, and used their predictions to justify staying on a course similar to the one that had been successful over the last 10 years. Neither side inquired into why the others saw the future differently. The CEO had the last say, declaring that further discussion would be a waste of time.

The conversation above is a composite of many such conversations I have observed over time. I have heard all the specific arguments made by individuals in this conversation many times. Just like the impasse they reached, the statements they made are real, not imaginary.

Strong Advocacy Usually Backfires

Here is the pattern that I see at the heart of most of these discussions. People who believe strongly in sustainability issues often unleash their energy in direct attempts to convince others of their views. They predict a very negative future ahead unless there is a significant change in course. They then forcefully advocate one or more "big bets" based on their personal prediction. These might be large investments in new technologies, production facilities, materials or processes that would leave a smaller environmental footprint, or "green" marketing campaigns that might lead the market or force a commitment from the rest of the enterprise or industry. Their intent is to provoke immediate and large-scale change.

But such sustainability champions generally get the opposite results. The executive team discounts their prediction, resists any significant change, and often takes no action at all, not even placing a "small bet" to learn more about the issue together or start a small pilot venture. Even worse, the advocates miss an important opportunity to enroll the entire leadership team in a conversation about the broader future of the company. Such a conversation could lead to a fresh start, a chance to engage the whole organization with high collective ownership and commitment.

Engaging key decision makers in a more productive conversation requires a clear strategy for engagement. Having passion about big issues is not enough. Being "right" can backfire. I find that the most consistent point of energized connection for line business leaders is the commercial viability and economic sustainability of the firm. That is where they have a stake. If you attempt to engage them in a more isolated conversation about the environment or social responsibility, they will tend to see that as a very narrow, perhaps trivial slice of the future—one that is only marginally relevant to the core of the business and its viability. Their past mental models—that these issues should be delegated to specialists to "take care of them and keep them out of our hair so we can get on with business"—reinforce this perception.

A second key criterion for an effective engagement strategy: It must improve the quality and capacity of the team's thinking about the future, and the quality of relationships and interactions between the participants as they think together. This is not a one-shot conversation, and any effective step forward in engagement will lead to others. Building the team's capacity to keep digging deeper is paramount. One-time "victories" for sustainability advocates that leave bitterness and polarization are a classic example of winning the battle but losing the war.

STEP ONE:
Seeing past the big bets—An initial conversation

What can you do to make an engagement successful? People like you in your role as CFO (or VP of IT, R&D, or other roles that are one step removed from the heat of the conflict between advocates) can play a crucial role in helping the senior team step back from promoting their specific predictions about narrow slices of the future, and engage in a much wider conversation about a full set of futures that could have a large impact on the company. In doing this, you will be making an essential contribution to the team by creating a new forum within which a truly generative inquiry can occur about unknowns in the future, with all members of the team fully engaged and contributing valuable new insights from their unique vantage points.

If you are in the role of the VP of strategy, you are in an ideal position to propose that such a dialogue occur as part of the planning cycle. You can set aside time for meetings that focus on the future, including time horizons from one to at least five years out, and can likely get support for a one-time excursion farther out into the future—ideally, 15 to 25 years. You can suggest that this time horizon at least match the replacement cycle for your capital assets.

It is usually not difficult to set aside some quality time for thinking about the future if you position the benefits clearly. If necessary, enlist support for allocating this agenda time from members of the team who are not directly involved in heated advocacy. You can also ask them to help you ensure that the conversations are broad enough to be relevant to all members and to the entire scope of the business, not just slices of it, like environment and social responsibility. These issues will be seen by many members as narrow stovepipes that should be handled by the functional VPs responsible for those areas. Fine-tuning an implementation plan involving how to position public announcements to appease your strongest critics in the environmental and social justice movements, for example, may end up being the responsibility of the VP of EHS. Unfortunately, the hand-off usually happens at the end of the decision pipeline, after the important business decisions have been made.

I will outline here a relatively simple first step that involves four basic questions for leadership teams, which can combat the myopia of their single-forecast approach to the future. I will later recommend the use of a broader, more robust process based on developing a full set of driving forces and scenarios. But here is a simple team process that can definitely help as an initial step, and can build commitment to going further with scenario work.

This approach works best if the team engages an unbiased, credible person to run the meeting. This could be the VP of strategy or a different member of the strategy team, another member of the senior team who is a good facilitator and will ensure full participation by everyone, or even a respected board member from another company.

The first question is "What are our assumptions?" and the first goal of the meeting is to unearth all the assumptions underlying your strategies for the future. Here are some assumptions of the electric utility: Ample long-term (20-year) supplies of coal, oil, and gas will continue to be available at prices similar to today's. Climate change concerns and associated taxes or penalties for CO_2 production will not materialize over the next 10 to 20 years.

An airline company's strategy might be based on the assumption that carbon taxes will not materialize. In addition, company executives might assume that in the unlikely event that such taxes are implemented, airlines will continue to fly freely above any national or international agreements and be exempt. (It's worth noting that Richard Branson of Virgin Atlantic Airlines seems to be hedging against a different assumption, and is actively exploring investments in large-scale ethanol production from crop and forestry waste.)

Once all assumptions and mental models about the future have been posted where everyone in the meeting can see them, the first question has been answered. The second question is "How do our current strategies serve us if these assumptions change?" The third question is "What options could we create and invest in over time that would improve the robustness of our overall portfolio of strategies in the event that these assumptions change?" I find that participants naturally gravitate to these or similar questions, as the prior exploration of assumptions generates a lot of tension that they want to resolve through further work together. Once your team sees how their current strategies are affected by changes in some of the key assumptions on which they are based, they will want to examine how significant those impacts are, and in what areas.

That exploration, in turn, creates energy for tackling the final question, "What should we be doing now so that we are more prepared if these assumptions change?" Direct the team's attention to generating options (often small bets focused on becoming more knowledgeable about particular areas of vulnerability and the surrounding territory). Emphasize a more open, creative process here, going for quantity of ideas first, then narrowing them down to a set of options that each have an owner or sponsor from the senior team. These sponsors take ownership for fleshing out the actions needed to develop each option and monitor changing external business conditions relevant to that option.

STEP TWO: Identifying driving forces

A valuable second step to take that will build on the momentum of the initial process above is to ask "What are the deeper forces that are driving the assumptions we identified?" From the conversation on surfacing assumptions, you will have already begun to identify some of these. For example, in considering the forces that might drive international climate change agreements and carbon taxes, you may have identified three separate forces that need to be understood and monitored over time, both separately and together:

1) scientific opinion and objective current data about global warming, including subtle measures like small changes in ocean temperature

2) physical changes in climate, weather, and storms that citizens can see and experience directly

3) public attitudes toward and perceptions of climate change: You may have already noted that the public has a mixture of concerns about local air pollution; concerns about regional accumulation of toxins like PCBs and mercury in air, water, and soil; and global concerns about greenhouse gases. (Most citizens don't know the scientific distinctions between these factors. Survey research shows that people see them as a single cluster of effects that are all bad for the health of their children.)

In looking at the assumptions you might have made about the impact of China on markets and pricing for oil, gas, metals, and other commodities, you may have identified the driving force of the race for economic growth in China, the desire of the Chinese to establish their dominance and make the country the global center of manufacturing, with all the accompanying implications for wealth creation in China and global financial dominance (and perhaps political dominance as well). Those driving forces are inescapably intertwined with bottom-up pressures in Chinese society for social change toward democracy.

Once your team has identified a full list of driving forces, you can extend the dialogue into exploring each one more fully and categorizing them with regard to their degree of impact on your business (low versus high impact). For example, breakthroughs in biotechnology that could extend human life might have high impact for a health-care insurer, low impact for a global oil company—but be careful here. Biotech could also have high impact for an oil company through the development of generic enzymes that can digest thousands of tons of waste daily, and create alternative feedstocks or materials for producing plastics and fuels.

Once you have sorted the driving forces into two lists—those with low and high potential impact on your business—sort each of those lists again into two subsets: those for which the outcome is certain and those for which outcomes are uncertain. For example, you can predict the number of native 25-year-olds living 20 years from now with relative certainty from the number of 5-year-olds today. Predicting net immigration patterns may be more uncertain, driven by global events beyond your country's borders.

For those driving forces that are relatively certain, you can rely more heavily on forecasting and build your plans accordingly. For those that are highly uncertain and also high impact, it is dangerous to have only one set of plans and strategies. It is most crucial, then, to focus in on those driving forces.

For example, here are the two most crucial driving forces identified by a team from an energy company (I will call it Futures Energy to protect the innocent) with strategic interests in building a broad portfolio of investments in power generation and transportation fuels, and a future strategy to extend into specialty chemicals. The two potential extremes for each of these forces are shown at left and right.

Cultural Values and Response Patterns

Exclusive cultural values		Inclusive cultural values
Win/lose		Win/win
Protectionist	$\longrightarrow$	Holistic
Linear		Systemic
Have and have-nots		Global mindsets

State of the Natural Environment

Changes in the environment
are of low urgency

$\longrightarrow$

Changes in the environment
require urgent response

Note that the mandate for this team's work was clearly focused on the long-term growth and viability of the business over the next 35 years. It was not focused in any way on the environmental and social dimensions of their strategy. Yet the societal issues of cultural inclusiveness and the urgency of environmental challenges surfaced in the course of the discussion as having the highest impact and most uncertain driving forces. If you are a believer in the importance of sustainability considerations, you can have faith that people will find their own connections between their current world and sustainability, if you give them a clear, unbiased process for exploring the future.

A team from a different company in the chemical industry (let's call it Scenario Chemicals) chose the following two driving forces as the most uncertain and highest impact for their business over the next 25 years. Again, the two extremes are displayed for each of the driving forces.

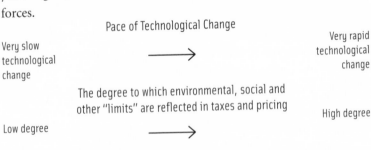

Pace of Technological Change

Very slow
technological
change

$\longrightarrow$

Very rapid
technological
change

The degree to which environmental, social and
other "limits" are reflected in taxes and pricing

Low degree

$\longrightarrow$

High degree

Again, future impacts of sustainability considerations (e.g., social and environmental driving forces) came up naturally as crucial factors affecting the core business, and were validated by all participants in an open, consensus-based process.

Both teams derived substantial new insights by considering the impacts that these top two driving forces could have on their business.

Futures Energy immediately began to monitor these forces for early signals on their direction. For example, within six months of company executives' initial work, they began to see signs of systemic thinking appearing in unusual coalitions on U.S. energy policy, at the federal, regional, state, and local levels. Here are a few paragraphs from a bellwether article that surfaced in their scanning of news media from *The Globe and Mail* newspaper on November, 17, 2005:

Spooked by the post-Katrina gas price spike, the U.S. Congress has suddenly found the religion of conservation.

A broad and powerful coalition of lawmakers—from environmentalists to fundamentalist Christians—introduced sweeping legislation yesterday that aims to cut U.S. oil consumption in half by 2031 and would require that half of all cars sold be fuel-miserly hybrids within a decade.

"There was a mental sea-change that we saw in America when gasoline hit $3 (U.S.) a gallon," explained Republican Senator Sam Brownback, one of the bill's co-sponsors.

Democratic Senator Joe Lieberman warned that the United States risks becoming a "pitiful giant" unless it curbs its dependence on foreign oil, which accounts for two-thirds of the roughly 20 million gallons a day the country consumes.

"We will become like Gulliver in Lilliput, pegged down and subject to the whims of those smaller nations because we are giving them, by our own consumption patterns, the ropes and helping them tie the knots that keep us down."

The legislation includes tax breaks of up to 35 per cent to get fleet operators to buy hybrid gas-and-electric or alternative fuel vehicles. It would also provide loan guarantees to get auto makers to move from producing gas guzzlers to making lightweight and fuel-efficient autos, as well as new incentives for bio-fuels, such as ethanol and cellulose biomass. . . .

The Futures Energy team also began to sketch systems diagrams to reflect this emerging systemic perspective. One example, using the shifting the burden archetype as the template, follows.

This archetypal pattern represents the tendency of any system to seek balance. It includes a lower loop that represents a fundamental long-term solution—in this case, to increase investments in energy efficiency and new technologies, which, as they mature, reduce demand for energy; create alternative domestic energy sources (such as ethanol, wind, and solar); and achieve balance by reducing dependency on imports of foreign oil. As with all other investments of this kind, these will take time to come to fruition.

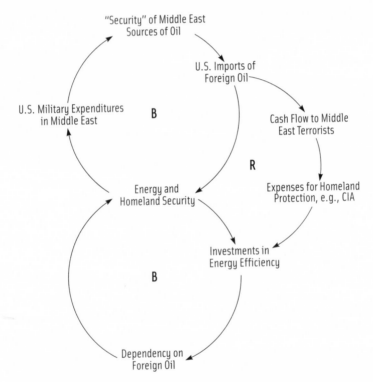

The upper loop represents a shorter-term solution, and one that appears easier to implement, at least at the outset. The intent here is to use military measures to secure Middle East sources of oil, so that U.S.

imports can rise to balance growing demand. Strategies that attempt to achieve balance through this upper loop often have an addictive effect; as growing energy needs are met in this way, the U.S. becomes more and more dependent on oil from the Middle East. It is this pattern that Senator Lieberman aptly described above. Often, nasty side effects accompany this addictive pattern and make matters worse. Here a vicious circle comes into play—a portion of the cash flows that are directed to the Middle East in payment for oil are channeled to terrorist organizations. In defense, the U.S. has to redirect funds to homeland security measures that could instead have been used to support R&D and new technologies. Side effects like these weaken the ability of the system to pursue fundamental long-term solutions, and increase dependence on short-term fixes.

Monitoring trends and patterns like these can allow you to adjust your strategies much earlier than your competitors, as you will be attuned to the possibilities of their emerging, and will be proactively looking for them. In addition to monitoring, the next stage to derive value from your work on high-impact driving forces is to use them to "stress test" or "wind tunnel test" your strategies in each of the extremes you have identified. How do your strategies allow you to compete if you imagine you are doing business at the extremes of these variables? If you find you do poorly or are out of business in any of those situations, then create options that allow the company to survive and thrive no matter which way the driving forces play out.

STEP THREE: **Creating scenarios**

Once the most crucial and uncertain driving forces have been identified and explored, a valuable third step is to create scenarios that portray a set of imaginative but plausible stories about the varied ways in which the world might turn out tomorrow. This step allows your team to combine the implications of several driving forces into distinct stories. You are then free to imagine how multiple forces might interact systemically within one possible future, in line with how the real world actually works. We don't have the luxury in the real world of looking at one variable alone (like technological change) while holding all other variables constant! In creating scenarios, as in real life, it is the surprising systemic interdependencies between events and forces that make life interesting—and highly unpredictable.

For example, at Futures Energy, the team first explored the two scenarios that emerged when changes in the environment required urgent responses.

In their view, virtually none of their current strategies were viable in these worlds. When cultural values were holistic and systemic, the team envisioned a world in which "we survive the storm together—barely." Given the scale, scope, and urgency of responses needed, they saw that it took all hands on deck on spaceship Earth, working systemically, to get through the crisis. At the other end of the scale, when they imagined that prevailing cultural response patterns were win/lose and protectionist, they saw a world of scarcity, conflict, and "subsistence of the fittest." Basic survival became the goal of citizens. Quality of life in the developed world dropped well below current standards. The team also portrayed the impacts of a flu pandemic (labeled "quarantine world") that pushed fear and protectionism to an extreme and created a major economic depression due to health-related barriers to trade and travel.

Using these scenarios as provocation, the Futures Energy team recognized that they needed to generate and invest in a much wider range of options than they had been considering until then, including a broad swath of renewable energy technologies and applications. Initially many of these options required the placement of small bets relative to the company's size. These ranged from $10,000 to $100,000 and were primarily focused on accelerating their scanning, learning, and testing of a portfolio of options. Today, as the company learns more, it is ramping up its investments—in some cases to much bigger bets, particularly where early indications are that some of the modeled scenarios are actually materializing.

Scenario Chemicals, similar to Futures Energy, focused initially on a future in which social, environmental, and other limits would drive high taxes and high materials prices at every step of their value chain. When this was coupled with rapid technological change, they saw themselves in a very leaky, flimsy boat in a "continuous whitewater world." They concluded that they had very weak capabilities to respond to this world. They saw that they would be taken out by innovative new competitors with a much cheaper replacement product that had the same or better functionality and a radically reduced environmental footprint.

Conversely, with the pace of technology change being slow, they could foresee a world they called "the big squeeze" where they would be driven into a loss position with no technological innovations to allow them to break free.

The team aligned quickly on the need to create and actively invest in three separate innovation options that would allow them to prosper in these scenarios. They moved forward immediately on these three options:

1. Ramping up staffing and budgets in R&D, focusing on creating new innovative products before nimble competitors, and agreeing to propose acquiring one of those small competitors if they deemed that it was the most cost-effective way to make progress.

2. Charging a high-profile team with creating a breakthrough in their manufacturing process that would cut capital and energy costs in half, and cut their footprint by more than half for any new plants to be built anywhere in the world.

3. Focusing a team on improving the capacity and productivity of their existing plants.

The first two teams are developing plans that will likely require a significant step up in the scope of the option they are working on—that is, they are developing proposals to move from a smaller bet to a much bigger bet as they further define the Stage Two investments needed and the size of the prize. They have maintained excellent top management interest and sponsorship for their efforts.

A Few Final Tips

As your team begins work on any of the steps outlined above, be sure to forewarn them that emotional tensions may run high as they explore the future, and prepare for this. Emotional reactions (like fear, anxiety, denial, and anger) are virtually unavoidable when you are exploring plausible stories about the future that include negative events. Your goal in the process is to step into those futures as if you are living there. If you do this wholeheartedly, you will almost certainly find yourself thinking about how you and your loved ones will fare in those worlds. The short answer in some futures will be "not well."

I notice that many leaders who participate in scenario planning end up developing their own family strategies and options for coping in difficult worlds. These might include becoming more involved in their local community to help make it more resilient, changing their personal investment strategies, or buying a remote cabin on a lake with a 100-acre woodlot and a wood-burning stove. So when emotional tensions run high, find a way to make them discussable so they can be honestly acknowledged as legitimate. Use those feelings to build candor, empathy, and spirit within your team, and then set them aside to once more focus on the work at hand. If you don't plan for this, your team will run out of energy, and you may not know why it has happened.

Certainly the steps I have suggested here require commitment, rigor, and the willingness to challenge assumptions and mental models, but they are worth the effort. For in the process of engaging the future together, leadership teams can develop a much more confident, proactive stance toward their collective future, and forge a deep commitment to address all aspects of the sustainability of the company—economic, environmental, and social.

Paradoxically, by exploring what might happen in the world that is beyond their control, teams will develop much more confidence about what they can control—their vision and the process of creating viable options and actions to realize that vision. And the original advocates for sustainability will land a bigger prize—the entire top team engaged in a rich set of stories about the future, naturally including the sustainability issues they might have advocated for in isolation. These issues will now be embedded in a much more inclusive picture, and fully integrated into the company's portfolio of strategies and options for the future.

Resources

Peter Senge, Art Kleiner, Charlotte Roberts, Rick Ross, Bryan Smith, *The Fifth Discipline Fieldbook*, Currency/Doubleday, 1994, pp 275-278

Peter Schwartz, *The Art of the LongView*, Currency/Doubleday, 1991

LEXICON

Sustainability

sus·tain·able

Function: adjective
1 : capable of being sustained
2 a : of, relating to, or being a method of harvesting or using a resource so that the resource is not depleted or permanently damaged <*sustainable* techniques> <*sustainable* agriculture> **b** : of or relating to a lifestyle involving the use of sustainable methods <*sustainable* society>
- **sus·tain·abil·i·ty** / noun [9]

Sustainable means capable of continuing indefinitely without depletion or diminished return.

The word sustain came into English with the Norman Conquest in 1066, from the Old French sustenir, "sustain," from Latin *sub-* "under," and *tenere* "to hold." Sustainable originally meant simply "capable of being endured" or "capable of being defended." But sustainable in the contemporary sense came into written use with the economics term *sustainable growth*. In 1965 the *McGraw-Hill Dictionary of Modern Economics* defined it as follows:

> **Sustainable growth:** a rise in per-capita real income or per-capita gross national product that is capable of continuing for a long time. A condition of sustainable economic growth means that economic stagnation will not set in.

One of the first uses of *sustainable* as an economic term can be found in a 1971 edition of the science journal *Nature,* in an article on the blue whale fishery: "The blue whale could have supplied indefinitely a *sustainable* yield of 6,000 individuals a year." That is to say, the business of whaling them *could have been* sustainable at that level; but once they had been over fished, the industry would die.

The first known use in print of the term *sustainability* was by Thomas Sowell in his book *Say's Law* (Princeton University Press, 1972). The book discusses the 19th-century economic theory of Jean-Baptiste Say, who argued that as long as prices and wages are perfectly flexible, a market will be self-regulating, and supply and demand will stay in sync. Regulation and minimum wages are the roots of all problems for Say; only free economies are sustainable. John Maynard Keynes disproved this optimistic theory in his 1936 *General Theory of Employment, Interest, and Money*, and kicked off modern economics in the process.

Today, when executives and financial analysts talk about the sustainability of a business, they are talking about the staying power of the business model, and the ability of the business to generate profit over time. In the strictest business sense, sustainability describes a business built to last a long time into the future.

The definition of sustainability coined in the book *Our Common Future*, published in 1987 by the United Nations' World Commission on Environment and Development (and also known as *The Brundtland Report*), introduced the business world to a new goal for economic development. Sustainability was defined as "[meeting] the needs of the present generation without compromising the ability of future generations to meet their own needs." This is the definition that has inspired a global movement of people from many walks of life to envision creative new strategies of economic development and to reduce societal strife and stress.

Other definitions put even more emphasis on regeneration—the power of generating, originating, producing, or reproducing. John Ehrenfeld, executive director of the International Society for Industrial Ecology, defines sustainability as "the possibility that all forms of life will flourish forever." For human beings, the term flourishing encapsulates not only surviving and maintaining the species but also a sense of dignity and authenticity.[10] Ehrenfeld and coauthor Sara Schley together offer a generative definition as it applies to business: "Sustainability in business means creating businesses as living systems in alignment with nature so all life can flourish for all time."

Materials Pooling: The Next Industrial Vision

Chris Page

The industrial world we live in consumes and produces a bewildering mix of raw materials and waste streams—natural and synthetic, benign and toxic, life preserving and life threatening. The life cycle of any single product in a supply chain can involve hundreds of chemicals, manufacturing processes, companies, and transactions. Increasingly, companies are compelled by regulation, public pressure, or internal governance to reduce or eliminate sources of toxicity and waste. However, it is often difficult to know where to start.

The need to tackle this challenge is exactly what inspired a diverse group of companies to launch a learning collaborative in 2001. This multi-industry partnership began exploring the possibilities for collaborating to more sustainably manage raw material flows in manufacturing. With the guidance of the SoL Sustainability Consortium and the Rocky Mountain Institute, participants have included representatives from Nike, Ford, BP, Unilever, Harley-Davidson, Hewlett-Packard, Plug Power, Aveda, Sikorsky, Pratt & Whitney, Visteon, and about 20 component and raw materials suppliers.

My own involvement in what is now called the Materials Pooling project began at the Collaborative Innovation for Sustainability meeting in Aspen, Colorado, in early 2002. Members of the SoL

Sustainability Consortium gathered for two days to share insights from their own sustainability efforts and to brainstorm future points of shared learning. Going into the meeting, we did not know what the outcome would be, but we were relatively confident that the mix of thoughtful and dedicated people present would produce some interesting results. Indeed, the seeds of the Materials Pooling working group were planted at that meeting. My ongoing participation with the project has been motivated and sustained by my working relationships with these people, at least as much as by the technical opportunities and challenges of materials pooling itself.

What is Materials Pooling?

In their book, *Cradle to Cradle: Remaking the Way We Make Things*, German chemist and former Greenpeace activist Michael Braungart and American architect William McDonough lay out a vision for an industrial system where there is no waste. In this system, "Products can be composed either of materials that biodegrade and become food for biological cycles, or of technical materials that stay in closed-loop technical cycles, in which they continually circulate as valuable nutrients for industry."[11] The ultimate goal is the replacement of the toxic, disposable substances that are ubiquitous in our industrial system with substances that are nontoxic, that are as functional as or better than the old ones, and that fit into the earth's natural order.

One strategy to achieve this vision is through what Braungart calls intelligent materials pooling. This is a collaborative partnership among multiple companies in which partners agree to share a common supply of high-quality materials, pooling information about these materials and their purchasing power. The result is a closed loop system that promotes healthy material flows. Braungart compares this to catch-and-release fly-fishing: Each angler catches the fish, treats it carefully as a valued resource, and releases it back in the pool it came from. Synthetic industrial substances become technical nutrients, or materials that flow, similar to nitrogen or water or plant matter, in a continuous cycle of life, regeneration, reuse, and regeneration in yet another form.

The vision is a compelling one; its actual execution is daunting. The idea of materials pooling had been around for several years when Michael Braungart mentioned to Peter Senge that he thought the Sustainability Consortium might have the right collection of companies and shared vision to implement the concept. When the idea was championed by a Nike representative at our Aspen meeting, we began to examine what it would take to begin such a process.

Tackling the Problem

On one level, the project's goal was to confront a fundamental technical challenge. How to replace materials of concern with environmentally preferred ones? How can we transition from a "take, make, waste" approach to design and manufacturing, to one in which we treat industrial material streams as valuable and renewable nutrients that can be reused? Even more importantly, how do we challenge and change people's mental models about what waste is, how recycling should work, and what value lies hidden in things we typically throw away?

Collaborative change projects, involving co-creation of common goals and team learning across a broad range of companies, represent an emerging, exciting, and extremely challenging business model. Some of our most important discoveries in the Materials Pooling project have involved seeing the opportunities for innovation and environmental improvements across industries.

Still, the deep level of inquiry, commitment of time, and sharing of knowledge required to achieve modest goals surprised even the most engaged participants. Although slow and laborious, such collaborations are essential to "operationalize" sustainability principles. Our group quickly realized that we needed to expand our discussion of what "materials pooling" meant to us. Our "pooling" involved intensive levels of sharing knowledge, coordinating strategy, wrangling our suppliers, and building trust long before we could begin pooling tangible supplies of preferred materials.

Our definition of materials pooling has expanded from Braungart's definition to include the activities of a broad range of actors in a network who are collaborating to reduce waste and toxicity across value chains, and develop a competitive advantage. In other words, materials pooling for us involved a network of players pooling their demand to influence the nature, quality, and availability of a more sustainable material supply desired by all.

The Big Tent

In order to identify specific materials around which we might collaborate, we organized a "big tent" brainstorming meeting for Consortium members and nonmembers. As we started to plan, we discovered that the reasons for participating in the project were as varied as the companies involved. Some members saw an opportunity to do something with a material they produced. Others, like Nike, were looking at ways to reduce toxic materials in their products; one of Nike's core corporate responsibility goals is to create products that are both innovative and sustainable. Other companies, such as Visteon, were feeling the pressure of impending regulations; in the European Union, manufacturers were facing the implementation of the E.U.'s "End-of-Life Vehicle (ELV) Directive," which drastically restricted use of materials such as lead and hexavalent chromium and placed stringent "take-back requirements" upon automotive companies and their suppliers. Among other requirements, the ELV Directive dictates that automobiles sold in Europe be 95 percent recyclable by 2015. Since it would be next to impossible to achieve such standards via "business as usual," ELV was forcing companies to look around for different approaches to business and product design innovation—including multi-industry collaboration—in order to fulfill these requirements.

After several months of planning with a core group of companies, our "big tent" meeting happened in December of 2003. We met in an enormous hangar at Pratt & Whitney headquarters. By the end of the two days, work groups had been established to address four materials platforms: corrugated shipping containers, hexavalent chromium, polypropylene, and leather. Other materials, including rubber and polyurethane, were of central concern to a single company, but lacked the critical mass of interest from multiple participants to support a useful collaboration.

Conversations over the two days took some unexpected turns. The leather group expanded its focus to include a much broader analysis of the state of leather. Coming into the meeting, the topics for conversation were the elimination of chromium from the leather tanning process, and the creation of demand for a synthetic leather that could be produced sustainably. As part of the development of the meeting's agenda, Vanessa Margolis of Nike challenged the group to look at other issues related to leather, questioning whether chromium was the only—or even the biggest—concern, and cited the importance of having dialogues with current and potential suppliers about reducing toxic materials in the overall production of leather, whether natural or synthetic. The group developed a map of the various environmental impacts throughout the life of a piece of leather, from problems of wastewater from manufacturing all the way through to safe end-of-life disposal of the product.

The polymers group, meanwhile, narrowed its discussion to examine the considerable potential for recapturing postindustrial polypropylene, a plastic resin often used in consumer packaging. The material has a very low recapture rate, so the group sketched out a value map to explore the various components of the polypropylene value chain. Matt Roman from Visteon pointed out the importance of not merely recapturing polypropylene, but meeting the challenge of acquiring high-quality recaptured polypropylene that could satisfy the high-performance specifications of the auto industry.

It was John Delfausse, vice president of packaging for the cosmetics company Aveda, who summed up the potential for polypropylene materials pooling in an anecdote that became a short and compelling story to orient newcomers to the goals of the group over the months that followed. Delfausse was touring one of Gillette's recycling facilities and noticed that the trays used for parts assembly were made from polypropylene—exactly the polymer he needed for his cosmetic caps. Aveda had committed to including recycled content in the caps. The trays, which were strictly for use within the factory, were purple. Why not make them clear, or even black? Delfausse's example challenged us to reframe the issue of waste: if we can engage with the entire supply chain and collaborate in designing a product upstream, "waste" downstream can become a valuable, useful feedstock for another company to use in its own products. If Gillette were to think of its purple trays as more than just trays, then Aveda could use them for their own product, and both companies would benefit.

As the months passed, the groups that had formed at the Pratt & Whitney meeting continued to convene by conference call and in person. It was helpful to watch partnerships form, and minor victories emerge along the way. I could almost always count on John Delfausse to happily inform me of the unexpected connection he had made, for example a new supplier for recycled plastic for his cosmetic caps. Matt Roman observed that he regularly had conversations within the auto industry about its challenges, but this forum was his one opportunity to speak with a diverse mix of companies like Nike, Harley-Davidson, and Unilever in order to gain their insights.

One of the core goals of materials pooling is creating a high-quality material stream for reuse. After several conference calls, the polypropylene group identified a two-pronged problem: a company like Visteon, which uses polypropylene to make dashboards for car manufacturers, has enormous demand for the polymer, but also has very high performance standards. Although there is a great deal of uncaptured polypropylene waste in the world, there is also little record of its quality or origin. Lacking that record, waste polypropylene couldn't be used to make dashboards. In pondering this problem, the group hit upon the notion of creating a system to record the history and origin of a feedstock of post-industrial polypropylene and assign it a "pedigree." With the pedigree, the buyer of the feedstock would know where the material came from, what it had been used for, and how it had been handled. The concept required a couple of key shifts in thinking, since treating a waste stream to retain or increase its value was a fairly drastic departure from the way waste had traditionally been handled.

Barriers to Collaboration

Although the idea of pooling the efforts, knowledge, and market demand of diverse companies around specific materials seemed like a straightforward idea, it was not; the further into the process we dug, the more we realized how much work lay ahead. The diversity of the companies was a strength when it came to brainstorming and high-level collaboration, but it proved more challenging when we sought common ground on very specific materials. The leather that Nike used in its footwear and the leather that Harley-Davidson used in its apparel were worlds apart; all leather, the group learned, is not created equal. Moreover, Nike's interest in exploring "green" synthetic leather had no traction with Harley-Davidson. One participant at the Pratt & Whitney meeting politely indicated that no Harley owner would be caught dead in a fake leather jacket.

In the subsequent months, we discovered further manifestations of the same problem. In the hexavalent chromium group, the search for a substitute material for chrome began to take us down divergent paths. Stainless steel met the performance needs of, say, Sikorsky for its helicopters. But the aesthetic difference between chrome and stainless steel on a Harley motorcycle would not be acceptable to the end customer.

Other challenges included:

Integrating Suppliers

Suppliers, of course, were a key part of understanding the barriers and opportunities a given material presented. However, suppliers also came with their own mental models and agendas. What if, for example, the best alternative to hexavalent chromium was a product that the supplier didn't make and would never make? What possible motivation would a supplier have to collaborate if that was the case?

Extracting information from suppliers about the characteristics of the materials proved difficult as well. The leather group and polypropylene group both formulated seemingly clear spec sheets for their suppliers to fill out regarding the nature of the product and the materials going into them. However, in many cases the supplier had no idea what toxic materials were in the product, and no incentive, financial or competitive, to find out what they were. On the off chance that a supplier did know what materials of concern were contained in its product, it had almost zero reason to share that information—particularly if the supplier suspected that the end result would be another hurdle or expense to deal with in order to keep a buyer happy.

Corporate support

The direct participants in the working groups also bore the burden of getting support from inside their companies. Only rarely was there a specific budget allocated to the Materials Pooling Project. As technical questions arose and project members had to seek the expertise of materials engineers and other specialists to answer questions, they encountered resistance. Harley's Hugh Vallely, who at the time was the Director of Motorcycle Product Planning (he has since retired), told us about a technical specialist from a Harley supplier complaining to him about research he'd requested: "I'm doing this without a charge code."

Often it was the few companies that had designated sustainability teams that did most of the heavy lifting. Companies like Nike and Unilever, which had already devoted the time internally to learn the complexities of such issues as packaging and leather processes, found themselves in the position of educating other companies further down the learning curve—but they were not necessarily learning or developing their own practices.

Competitive concerns

As we began to specify action steps and share information, anti-competitiveness regulations became a concern. How were we to get conversations beyond the level of generic discussion if there were legal prohibitions to discussing volume and price? If we couldn't engage in open exchanges with direct competitors, how could we move beyond an interesting brainstorming conversation into the specifics that would yield tangible results? A great deal of time was devoted to untangling where these new, collaborative activities fell with respect to the legal gray area of antitrust law—and how that law might, or might not, impede the development of a completely new business model for practicing sustainability. Typically, the diversity of our collaborative group meant that no direct competitors were involved in the conversation, nor was pricing part of our conversations. Still, the very fact that we were trying something entirely new required us to discuss these regulations in some detail.

A Critical Start

Regulations continue to be a significant factor in forcing corporations to reduce the environmental impacts of their operations. But one can argue that voluntary, market-driven, and cross-industry learning and action initiatives, such as the Materials Pooling project, hold the promise of yielding far greater and broader improvements than regulation alone can accomplish. Environmental challenges, and our understanding of potential ways to address them, are simply evolving too rapidly. Regulation cannot be expected to stay far enough ahead of new developments to effectively drive innovative solutions.

Whether participants stay engaged with the core Materials Pooling project, or strike out on their own to do other things, there is a palpable, spirited desire for innovation and an excitement in the discovery of new ideas among the people in this group.

One participant in the leather group, Nike's Margolis, has helped establish within the footwear industry an environmental stewardship assessment tool for tanneries. Currently, several footwear brands and tanneries are participating, with an expected release later in 2006. Using her experience from the project, Margolis is stimulating interest among peers she meets frequently at industry trade events. Sustainability may not even be on the agenda, but we all can see that having these face-to-face encounters with people who have a common language and industry knowledge makes it easier to get others who are not naturally crusaders for sustainability more interested in getting involved.

Seetha Coleman-Kammula, a chemical engineer and a relative late-comer to our materials pooling work, became intrigued with the polypropylene group's "pedigree" concept and spent considerable time advising us on the mechanics and opportunities of polymer recycling. Since then, she has developed several ideas related to various packaging polymers and, at the time of this writing, is helping to develop a new conceptual framework around sustainable product and process design.

John Delfausse, the VP of packaging from Aveda and a member of the polypropylene group, was for a short time involved with the Consortium's corrugated container effort, and then narrowed his focus to his core concerns about plastics and aluminum. Excited about sustainability in general, and inspired by the ideas of the polypropylene group, he is now engaging with a smaller number of suppliers to the cosmetics industry to develop recycled aluminum content for their packaging.

Visionaries such as Michael Braungart and William McDonough will continue to set the bar for what we can imagine is possible. But it is the work of the people who are willing to dig down into the messy details of the day-to-day operating realities that will make a sustainable future the sustainable present.

Reflecting on the process, Matt Roman wrote in a recent e-mail:

> The fundamental issue I encountered throughout this whole process pertained to a rather non-economic, non-scientific . . . notion of trust and relationships . . . We have set up our economic models around the concept of competition and the hoarding of information. But that is totally antithetical to what is needed when we are looking for material pooling. Even in situations such as this where we had a very non-competitive environment . . . we still found it very hard to share information (whether it was because we didn't think it worth our time to provide or because of competitive concerns). From that standpoint I think the Materials Pooling project was very successful

at identifying this as a key thing to work on in the future, how do we build trust among and across organizations to encourage the sharing of ideas and information for the betterment of us all. We have to keep working and practicing at this even if they fail to produce our intended results. I see it as the only way to break down those walls.

One of the overarching aims of the Sustainability Consortium is to nurture projects with long-term change goals in which companies work together to accomplish what they cannot do on their own. In this context, the Materials Pooling project is a model effort. Although the technological hurdles may loom large on the road to sustainability, getting people to wrap their minds around problems as complex as changing an industrial system, and doing it with passion and patience, is the critical start. Without it, change of any kind will never happen.

Resources

Kenneth Geiser, *Materials Matter: Toward a Sustainable Materials Policy*, MIT Press, 2001

Janine M. Benyus, *Biomimicry: Innovation Inspired by Nature*, Harper Perennial, 2002

William McDonough and Michael Braungart, *Cradle to Cradle: Remaking the Way We Make Things*, North Point Press, 2002

Etienne Wegner, *Cultivating Communities of Practice*, Harvard Business School Press, 2002

Art Kleiner, "Materials Witnesses," *strategy+business*, Spring, 2005

www.wasteonline.org.uk/resources/InformationSheets/vehicle.htm

www.wastewatch.org/uk

7

Seeding the Social Dimension at Schlumberger

Ann Graham

"It's common to say that trees come from seeds," write Peter Senge, Joseph Jaworski, Betty Sue Flowers, and C. Otto Scharmer in their book, Presence. "But how could a tiny seed create a huge tree? Seeds do not contain the resources needed to grow a tree. These must come from the medium or environment within which the tree grows. But the seed does provide something that is crucial: a place where the whole of the tree starts to form. As resources such as water and nutrients are drawn in, the seed organizes the process that generates the growth. In a sense, the seed is a gateway through which the future possibility of the living tree emerges."

This is precisely the concept that Simone Amber, a vice president of Schlumberger Ltd., has applied in order to become "a social entrepreneur inside a large company," as she puts it. Amber is the founder of Schlumberger Excellence in Educational Development (SEED) program. Organized within this 55,000-employee oilfield services multinational, SEED is an employee-run nonprofit that provides children from poor and remote communities in developing countries a chance to connect to the World Wide Web and thus to a wider world of science and technology.

Amber was raised in a comfortable middle-class setting in Beirut, Lebanon. She never lost her memory of seeing other children on the street selling candies so they could buy food. Leaving Lebanon on her own at 17 to finish high school in Paris, Amber later attended the Institute d'Etudes Politiques and received an MBA from INSEAD. "I was the first one in my family to go to university," she says. "I knew how important my education was, and I have always believed that there is great meaning to be found in using the opportunities you are given in life to help others."

Joining Schlumberger as an assistant treasurer for North America in 1985, Amber steadily moved up the corporate ladder, becoming director of investor relations and communications in 1994 and the head of marketing communications for a major business unit in 1999. In the mid-1990s, though, she began to feel restless. She wanted to do something more meaningful with her life than pursuing profit and financial security. Quoting John Gardner, she describes the kind of meaning she was looking for: something you "build into your life . . . out of your own past, out of your affections and loyalties, out of the experience of humankind as it is passed on to you, out of your talent and people you love, out of the values for which you are willing to sacrifice something."

She considered going to work for a nonprofit, but rather than leave Schlumberger, which she admired for its socially progressive culture, she saw the opportunity to cultivate something new from within. SEED is built on Schlumberger's unique workforce—people representing more than 145 different nationalities and operating in more than 100 countries, who have expertise in a range of scientific disciplines, and who are willing to share their knowledge and time as volunteers. Amber herself was SEED's first volunteer, working her day job in marketing and investor relations for four years while building up SEED's programs in her spare time, before becoming its full-time director in 2001. "The SEED philosophy is based on generosity," she says. "It is a unique opportunity for employees, who themselves have gained so much in their lives and careers with Schlumberger, to give something back and impact the next generation." (See SEED at a Glance, page 65.)

always had it in me to try to get the company involved in a social initiative like this. Back in the days when I was in treasury [at Schlumberger] I tried to push green investment. I had a friend who was doing sustainable forestry in tropical forests; he was really avant-garde. I was hoping we could make investments like this, but it was too crazy. Nobody inside the company would look at it.

In February 1993 I met Seymour Papert, a longtime researcher at the MIT Media Lab and one of the world's foremost experts on using technology for experiential learning. A friend of mine, an educator, wanted to meet him, and I had contacts at the Media Lab so I organized the meeting. I did not know Seymour Papert personally, and because I was curious I decided to go along. As it turned out, the meeting was really for me. After an inspiring conversation about Papert's work, I started telling him about my desire to capitalize on the resources of Schlumberger for a social purpose.

I had already decided to stay at Schlumberger, but I was still trying to figure out what I wanted to do there. Seymour introduced me to a project that he was involved in, bringing the Internet into a school in Costa Rica and a Boston inner-city school.

This meeting, and subsequent discussions with Seymour, helped me understand how we could leverage our company's competencies and how I could put form to my intent. The idea of SEED started to gel, but very slowly. In February 1994, I came back from a three-month maternity leave, and was promoted to director of investor relations. The company's results that year were difficult, so it required a great deal of work and sensitivity to deal with frustrated investors. I was also nursing my new baby. I was totally exhausted, emotionally and mentally. I didn't have a minute to think. In 1995 and 1996, however, I felt more settled in my job and I started talking again about my idea inside Schlumberger. We are a technology company with a depth of knowledge in science and technology. So focusing on science education made sense for us. I also knew we had the global reach and diverse international employee base to make SEED work. This company is the closest thing I have ever seen to the U.N. in corporate life. Plus, Schlumberger had had its own global intranet since 1985. That meant we had the IT infrastructure to reach the schools we wanted to reach.

Even though I had some credibility within Schlumberger, I didn't know anything about setting up educational programs. So I brought Seymour to meet with executives and test the waters. Ultimately, I knew I needed the CEO's approval to start anything. In 1997, I was finally ready to approach him. Our CEO at the time, Euan Baird, was a very reserved Scotsman; when he told me that he thought I had "a good idea" I knew he thought it was outstanding. I think that he saw its innovativeness, its fit with the company, and its potential value. But he didn't give me any money, and I still had to continue my day job. I didn't see this as a problem because there were people in the investor relations group who wanted to help. For example, the woman running the Schlumberger corporate Web site started creating the science education Web site that would serve as the portal for SEED on the Web. And I had enough money in my budget to pay a contractor once we got started.

We established SEED as a nonprofit foundation in 1998, but SEED is not really a foundation. We don't have an endowment, and we have never used our foundation status for tax purposes, because I would have had to hire someone to do the accounting. I simply wanted an umbrella that would allow SEED staff to work on projects. Since it's all funded internally, we didn't need to raise any funds. Today SEED has a $5 million annual budget. I control half of it. The rest comes from different country operations. Our research centers also fund some of the people on my team.

Initially, we approached a few country managers to help us identify some schools where we could provide our first Internet connectivity grants. They were willing to help, and that got us off the ground.

In 1999 I got another promotion, to vice president of marketing communication, for the test and transactions business unit. I continued to work on SEED as a volunteer until 2001, when the CEO called me into his office and asked if I'd like to work on SEED full time. We had been playing with the idea for a few months but I was not sure it would happen. I took the job immediately. I assume that he was curious to see how SEED could evolve if I were focusing on it fully.

Now that SEED is well established, I sometimes forget how hard it was in the early years. There were many days when I thought we would never get anything going. I learned to be patient and to persevere; it is an aspect of my personality I had to develop. My boss at the time, the vice chairman, would joke: "You kick her out the door, she comes back through the window." I think any entrepreneur must have this quality, and I see myself as a social entrepreneur. Inside our big multinational company, we had the feeling of a start-up.

In retrospect, there are eight main approaches that I think have helped us succeed: being a good navigator; living the company's values; keeping the intiative authentic; growing slowly; attracting people with passion; letting go of the business case; letting people pursue what they care about; and realizing that companies are human.

Being a Good Navigator

I'd had two big corporate jobs. They were platforms that allowed me to get to know the company in its totality; they also gave me credibility and contacts with key decision makers. Having given me a huge responsibility to represent the company on business matters, the CEO knew I wasn't a flake. He could see that I was serious.

To make a project like this work, you need to be able to navigate the system. You need to discern who to talk to and how to talk to them. The first few country managers who stepped up to the plate for us made a big difference, but I didn't know them well when I approached them—I might have met them a couple of times at a company gathering. Still, I sensed that they might respond positively. I never felt the need to go to them with a formal presentation; I just called them and explained the idea over the phone. I still do outreach this way. Country managers change jobs a lot so I have to constantly reinforce [existing] relationships and forge new ones.

Living the Company's Values

The program works because it is consistent with the values of the founding brothers, Conrad and Marcel Schlumberger. When I was head of investor relations, I visited with one of Conrad's daughters. She showed me correspondence between her father and her mother during the First World War. I could see her father was very concerned about the well-being of his soldiers. He wrote to his wife about how he had organized a recreational area for them. It sounds trivial, but the care he had for his people came through. He was also very humble. In one letter he told his wife that he had received a medal for his heroism as a soldier but would never put it on. "How can I wear it, when I know that some of my guys died or are now handicapped?" When I heard his daughter speak about her father—his humanism, open-mindedness, and tolerance for different kinds of people and cultures—I identified with how those qualities still persist in the company today.

Keeping the Initiative Authentic

In 1993, when I got the idea for SEED, CSR [corporate social responsibility] was not yet on the map as a management discipline. Today there are many more professionals within companies who are developing a company's social initiatives. If I had had that support then, it would have been easier. We wouldn't have had to start from scratch the way we did. Although SEED is definitely a social responsibilitysuccess story that could easily get more press attention, we deliberately haven't promoted the program in the media, or through other external marketing channels. Because we are a business-to-business company, external reputation value is not nearly as significant as it would be if we were a consumer products company. The real value for us is putting our resources behind internal promotion and getting more of our employees involved.

Growing Slowly

I know that the participation in SEED still involves a very small proportion of Schlumberger's employees worldwide. And it is not like we went from zero to a $5 million budget in one day. Ours has been slow, steady growth. But each year, we are reaching new milestones and expanding our capabilities. In December 2005 we passed the 1,500 volunteers mark. We have about 365 employees signed up to answer questions on the "Ask the Expert" part of the Web site. They're not active all the time, but they're signed up for it. The Connectivity Grant program in each country has at least one person who helps coordinate relationships with the schools, and lots of people locally help with the workshop projects. There are probably 200 to 300 people working in the field at any given time.

We are currently building an information database on volunteers' experiences. We use the Web site and the database to keep volunteers connected to our community, and to recruit and to grow the program in other ways. With the database we can measure our progress and growth, which is wonderful.

Attracting People with Passion

Being a volunteer initiative means attracting people because of their interest and passion. Many people work for SEED on weekends and during vacations, although they can also volunteer during regular work hours. SEED has never been a part of our formal business objectives. One country manager decided to make it an objective for his personnel function, but he is one out of 40. Keeping SEED going is all about individual motivation and teamwork. I have no direct power. I just do my best to inspire and convince people to help make SEED a success. I measure my own performance by setting my own objectives, for example, connecting 20 new schools a year and hosting 12 workshops, etc. But I have to go to my team, as well as to each country manager, to make this happen.

Would it be better for SEED to be part of the management performance system so we could attract more people and work with more schools? I'm not sure, but I know that people commit to SEED because it matters to them. I guess my decision to start SEED the way I did has evoked a similar desire in other people.

Letting Go of the Business Case

In the beginning I thought I needed to build a business case, but social objectives aren't something you can define as a traditional business "deliverable" in the same way you can position an environmental objective, for instance, as something that will reduce costs or risk.

Eventually I gave up trying to make the business case, and I felt relieved when I did. Today I can talk about business cases, but I'm usually not the one making them. Managers see the positive impact SEED has on their community relations, and they tell us what they think. Recruiters love it because lots of young people care about this issue, so it helps us present ourselves as a really interesting company.

Letting Employees Pursue What They Care About

Our managers travel a lot, and they hear people talking about SEED and see for themselves what we have done. I think this has made top-level management realize how much people care. Employees are giving their time to SEED, because it is very important to them. This employee motivation has become a business case that motivates managers to give the financial support that allows people to participate.

Realizing Companies Are Human

You often hear talk about companies as monsters, but a company is also a community of people. We are building a strong sense of community inside Schlumberger. I have learned that there is enormous untapped potential inside corporations. If we engage people in something that has meaning to them and that also uses their skills, we can have a huge impact on their lives and on the success and strength of the company and the community.

SEED at a Glance

In the middle of the Limoncocha Biological Reserve in Ecuador, two students at the village elementary school huddle in front of the computer screen in their "virtual" classroom, which opened in January 2005. The computer technology installed in this and four other schools in Ecuador gives 400 students, and their teachers, access to an online library where they can learn how to use the Internet and learn about Amazonian cultures in surrounding communities. At www.seed.slb.com, one can see SEED's vision come alive in a site brimming with photographs of smiling and inquisitive schoolchildren, and their teachers, from 36 countries throughout Asia, Africa, Latin America, and the Middle East.

Founded in 1998 as a nonprofit organization, the Schlumberger Excellence in Educational Development (SEED) program uses the World Wide Web and the resources and infrastructure of the multinational oilfield service company Schlumberger Ltd. to promote understanding among people from diverse cultures and deliver a variety of project-based learning experiences in science and technology to youths in developing countries. SEED's programs and resources are targeted to students ages 10 to 18 who live in the world's economically challenged communities.

SEED has four components:

- The School Network Program provides direct funding and technical assistance that enables schools to purchase computers with Internet access. As of December 2005, these grants have helped to wire 153 schools, reaching 170,000 children in 36 countries.

- The SEED public Web site is available in seven languages: Arabic, Chinese, French, English, Portuguese, Spanish, and Russian. The site's Online Science Center offers dozens of applications and exercises students can use on their own, or teachers can use in the classroom. Design Your Own Universe, for example, is a software tool that simulates the evolution of the universe and allows users to control the factors that determine the outcome. In the "Ask the Expert" section, Schlumberger employee volunteers—mathematicians, engineers, earth scientists, geologists, petroleum and mechanical engineers—answer questions submitted to them by kids using the site. More than 200,000 visitors come to the Science Center each month. The site is also referenced and used by 128 peer science Web sites in diverse countries, including the American Association for the Advancement of Science.

- Through the Web site, SEED has created an interactive global community of students and teachers who work on collaborative projects. For instance, student teams post reports about their water quality and availability on a global message board. Some choose other locally relevant projects, such as waste disposal in Ho Chi Minh City, Vietnam, or the underwater world of mangrove swamps outside Bangkok, Thailand. Students from anywhere in the world can read these reports and make comments. Collaborative projects help students develop research and communication skills and stimulate cross-cultural understanding and curiosity.

- Educational workshops led by SEED staff, Schlumberger employee volunteers, and partners from the Future of Learning Group at MIT's Media Lab use simple but creative teaching tools to engage students in understanding and solving social and environmental challenges in their communities. SEED School workshops are also led by Schlumberger scientists who spend anywhere from a few days to two weeks working with students at a SEED School.

In addition to the director, SEED has a staff of nine full-time employees who work on developing content for the programs, building relationships, growing the volunteer base, and other operational responsibilities. Staffers typically are experienced SEED volunteers who take on a SEED assignment for one to three years before rotating back into their traditional career track. The volunteer base for SEED includes employees, their spouses and children, and retirees. Since SEED's inception through 2005, 1,500 people have participated in the program.

Resources

Presence: An Exploration of Profound Change in People, Organizations, and Society by Peter M. Senge, C. Otto Scharmer, Joseph Jaworski, and Betty Sue Flowers, Doubleday/Currency, 2005; www.solonline.org/publications

Schlumberger, Ltd.: www.slb.com

Schlumberger Excellence in Educational Development: www.seed.slb.com/en/

The Future of Learning Group at the MIT Media Lab: http://learning.media.mit.edu/

The MIT Media Lab $100 Laptop: http://laptop.media.mit.edu/

The MIT Media Lab has launched a new research initiative to develop a $100 laptop for distribution to children around the world. To achieve this goal, a new nonprofit association, One Laptop Per Child (OLPC), has been created. The initiative was first announced by Nicholas Negroponte, Media Lab chairman and cofounder, at the World Economic Forum at Davos, Switzerland, in January 2005.

8

The Sustainability Engineer

Ann Graham

Erika Herz, the sustainability manager for UTC Power, LLC, a unit of United Technologies Corporation (UTC), is one person among hundreds with a job dedicated to integrating environmental and social perspectives into business decision making. Herz represents a new generation of MBAs helping to define sustainable management concepts and put them into practice in a large industrial company.

She is a graduate of the Darden Graduate School of Business Administration at the University of Virginia, which in 2005 was ranked among the top 30 schools in Beyond Grey Pinstripes. *This biennial survey and ranking of business schools by the Aspen Institute Business and Society program and the World Resources Institute highlights the pioneering efforts of business schools and individual faculty to integrate social and environmental topics into core curricula and research.*

At my Quaker high school in Pennsylvania, students were required to do a two-week service project in order to graduate. I got a scholarship to spend the summer in China. We took Chinese language classes in the morning, and in the afternoons we worked in the fields with the local farmers. Talking and working with people who were struggling just to eke out a living reinforced my conviction that I had a responsibility to use my education to help address social and environmental problems in the world.

After college, my husband and I taught English in Japan for two years. On our return to the U.S., we took the Trans-Siberian Railroad from Beijing to Moscow. I looked out the window and saw devastating erosion. Topsoil was swirling in the air, being blown off miles and miles of fields. Because he was so troubled by what he saw, my husband (who had been a foreign affairs major) decided to become a soil scientist, which is what he does now. That train trip was the first time that the global nature of pollution and environmental degradation really hit home for me.

When I was 32 years old, I chose to get my MBA at Darden because it had a strong commitment to sustainability. It was one of the dean's six priority initiatives. While I was there, I was also copresident of Students for Responsible Business. In that role, I had a chance to meet with business owners who had a sustainability focus, and to provide sustainability education for students.

Now, at 37, I am the sustainability manager for UTC Power, which makes fuel cells for transportation and on-site power markets, as well as other distributed-generation products for on-site power applications. I report to the director of operations and supply chain management.

This is the most cross-functional role I have had. I am in charge of examining all of our processes and products from the "triple bottom line" perspective. For us, that means making business decisions that consider not only the economic impact to the company, such as simple payback analysis, but also social and environmental impacts, the consideration of which requires a more sophisticated approach.

One of my major tasks is to determine the environmental "footprint" of all our products. We sell fuel cells and other combined cooling, heating, and power (CCHP) products, which have a much higher efficiency than grid power. However, we still need to understand the impact of the materials used to build our products, the energy used to run them, and the waste generated when we dispose of them at the end of life. Life cycle analysis (LCA) tools are helpful to accomplish this. An LCA analyzes an entire system, including material and energy flows. The goal is to use the information gleaned to continue to make product enhancements. Ideally, our products would be "zero-to-landfill" and carbon-neutral—adding no additional CO_2 to the atmosphere.

We grapple all the time with the practical challenges involved in pursuing these goals. For example, most people think of fuel cells as an environmentally friendly product, but it's not that simple. For example, most fuel cells run on hydrogen, so you have to look at how the hydrogen is made. Often hydrogen is made from electrolysis, which separates hydrogen and oxygen from water, and requires electricity. If your electricity is made from a polluting, coal-burning process, fuel cells do not look as good from an LCA perspective as if the hydrogen were produced using renewable energy. Also, some fuel cells are manufactured using platinum, and the environmental and social impact of mining is a major concern. Almost all of the platinum in fuel cells is reclaimed and reused, but this is just one example of how we need to approach product design and development very thoughtfully in order to be a sustainable company.

I'm also involved with marketing, which includes devising how to talk to customers about where we stand on sustainability and why we think it's important for them to embrace a sustainability mind-set. We share our conception of the triple bottom line with our customers and talk to them about how it is a different perspective.

Another aspect of my job is to educate employees internally about sustainability and environmental issues. UTC is a big company. If our communication about sustainability actually helps our 220,000 employees change their behavior, that is a big impact just from internal company communication.

One of our designers attended a meeting on green product design, and as a result, a sustainability metric has been added to our design software. Now when we are designing a part, we might ask the question "Is this part going to be recyclable?" A small thing like that gets people thinking. It also makes them more aware of the fact that, in some cases, we have to change. Because of new legislation, American companies will eventually be unable to sell products in Europe that contain lead. Making circuit boards without lead requires technology changes, but the new legislation makes it imperative that companies innovate if they intend to market products in Europe.

Although our sustainability work started slowly, it is steadily gaining momentum. Since 2002 I have been involved in the UTC Sustainability Network, which I now lead. It started with a handful of employees from different divisions who got together to talk about sustainability issues and put on educational seminars for leaders in the company. In December 2003 our chairman, George David, spoke at the SoL gathering hosted at UTC that our network helped organize. It gave a lot of credibility to sustainability efforts to have the chairman of UTC give a keynote presentation.

Practicing sustainability is challenging. Sometimes we don't have the technical answers, and that can be discouraging. But people are working on it. Large suppliers of electronics components are now required by their customers to provide lead-free products, for example. This is a beginning. Once a company is being pressured by its customers and by legislation to find solutions, then it is going to find them. Despite the challenges, there is nowhere else I would rather be than here, focusing my work on helping create a better planet.

9

Creative Development in Rural Africa

Bryan Smith and Sue Simington

When Nabasita Felicita was born 15 years ago, in a small village in the "lost counties" of Kibaale district in Western Uganda, her family lived in a two-room mud-and-wattle hut. She spent her days walking barefoot for miles to attend a poor-quality state school, listlessly sweeping their hut, weaving baskets to make a little money, or helping dig in their meager garden. Usually the family would cook cassava (a starchy root) in the morning, and eat it throughout the day, often cold.

In 1996, the parents of Felicita ("Nabasita" is her surname) and her two siblings abandoned them, leaving their grandmother to find a way to keep the family together and alive. It was a subsistence life; there was no hope for finding a way out of the family's grinding poverty. Graduating from primary school was expected to be the end of Felicita's formal education; the best future she could hope for was being married off into a more prosperous family.

Today, 15-year-old Felicita is a thriving high school student at a school for girls founded by an extraordinary locally based nongovernmental organization (NGO) called the Uganda Rural Development and Training Program (URDT). Indeed, Felicita's change of fortune parallels the successful work URDT has been doing to change the fortunes of everyone in a district where there had been only desperation, conflict, poverty, and many other seemingly insurmountable prob-

lems—a place of "silent violence," as described by URDT's three
founders, Silvana Veltkamp, Mwalimu Musheshe, and Ephrem Rutaboba.

URDT began its field operations in 1989, and Felicita's brighter
future is a direct result of the NGO's 17 years of steady growing impact
on the community. What is most notable about Felicita's experience is
that as a student of the URDT Girls School (established only five years
ago), she is now the change agent and leader for her family, teaching
her grandmother and siblings how to initiate specific development
projects for themselves. Her education represents the first real hope for
the family's future.

In the two years Felicita has been a student at the URDT Girls
school, her grandmother has been invited to come to the school near
the end of each term and has attended workshops for parents on a
range of subjects. Like most parents and guardians, she has made her
own way to the school, often on foot, to attend—motivated by her
pride in Felicita. She has learned about visioning, planning for the
future, entrepreneurship, innovation, home and farm improvement
projects, and business development. Like other students, Felicita leads
workshops for her grandmother and other students' parents on agricultural practices and home-improvement techniques she has learned
at school. Then they sit down together at the school and plan projects
for the family to do back home. Felicita's grandmother, Aidah, enthu-
siastically describes how their lives have been transformed, and how
they have participated in this transformation:

> Now we can cook many different foods. We cook three meals a
> day, at breakfast time, lunchtime, and dinnertime, and eat them
> warm. We eat many vegetables, like dodo [a kind of spinach]
> and eggplants, and fruits like pineapples. URDT has been guid-
> ing the whole development process of this family, through par-
> ents' workshops and the home visits made by the school–com-
> munity liaison. I have learned to work [as part of a] team, and
> how to improve our agricultural practices. My granddaughter
> helps in guiding me on what to do and how to do it best.

Such activities are emblematic of how URDT's approach takes a sharp turn away from the approaches of typical development agencies or community-based NGOs. URDT's philosophy is built on the theory that economic development won't happen as a result of, much less be sustained by, aid handouts: Sustainable economic development must come from the development of self-reliant individuals and communities that thrive locally. This means reducing dependency on grants by building up local income-producing businesses. Local people, not outsiders, envision the economic and social development goals they want to achieve, and work together to learn and practice the skills to achieve these goals. Typical aid-based development strategies may profess to tackle problems of poverty in a systemic way, but in reality, traditional projects, such as electrification of villages, the harvesting of medicinal plants, or the management of groundwater quality, are often conceived in a piecemeal fashion. In contrast, URDT has built an integrated development model designed with an understanding of the synergies and interdependencies among all initiatives.

Perhaps the most compelling piece of Felicita's story, and an affirmation of the effectiveness of the URDT model, is that her family's accomplishments represent the beginning of their emergence from the poverty trap. Western governments and multilateral institutions invest billions of dollars in aid and subsidies in emerging economies, but in sub-Saharan Africa, 600 million people still live on less than $3 per day. This poor Ugandan family who have a vision of how they will sustain themselves over the long term, all because of the successful intervention and support of one small intensive local development program.

Aidah's vision:

> I want to start a poultry project soon and I have already built the structure for it. Thieves stole my chickens the first time I tried to start the project, but I will start again. The URDT human rights officer helped me get the local police to investigate and let the suspected thieves know they are being watched. I don't think my chickens will be stolen again. I also want to be involved in a business in farm projects, and start a piggery. At

the end of every school term, I make sure that I am doing something to advance my situation.

I want to have a permanent structure for our house, and to have cattle. I have joined a parents' cooperative savings group to help put Priscilla (my other granddaughter) into school. I want all my grandchildren to be in good schools. I will do this by saving with a parents' group and doing well in business.

Felicita's vision: "If I study well, I expect I can be a doctor in the future."

The Five Disciplines in Rural Development

Established in 1987, URDT is the first NGO in Africa to apply the vision-based and holistic organizational learning and systems thinking approaches to human development. These disciplines were adapted for Uganda from the work of American consultant Robert Fritz and Innovation Associates (IA), the consulting firm cofounded in the 1970s by Peter Senge.

URDT's founders, Musheshe, Rutaboba, and Veltkamp, all with deep roots in Uganda and dedication and passion for doing rural development work there, spent time in the United States in the 1980s receiving training from Robert Fritz and IA. Musheshe and Rutaboba were young graduates from Makerere University who originally volunteered to join the project when Veltkamp and her husband decided to create it in Uganda. Veltkamp, born in Italy, raised in Africa, and living in the U.S., was an experienced development professional with the United Nations.

Veltkamp decided to found URDT with her husband, Han, after concluding that most aid programs were simply not working. She believed that with a different approach, real progress could be made. Veltkamp was particularly insistent that URDT be an indigenous voluntary organization that Ugandans would create and lead. She and Han provided early seed money and ensured that URDT's leaders received powerful training in new ways to think and take action—by working in the U.S. with Robert Fritz on personal mastery and with IA to absorb the organizational learning disciplines. No one could imagine then how powerful these concepts would become in the hands of the talented Ugandans who returned to their country and diligently applied what they had learned, transforming the concepts to work at the level of the entire Kibaale district, with its population of approximately 400,000, as well as at village and household levels.

Starting with villagers' energy and vision, URDT began to engage villagers in matters of the greatest interest and concern to them. In 1989, URDT leaders began holding informal gatherings that evolved into three-day workshops, following the visionary leadership and planning approach that IA had developed. They began with brief introductions to the concepts of personal and shared vision on day one, then immediately applied them so that the villagers created their initial vision for the village. The second day was devoted to explaining the concept of "current reality," and assessing what they had to work with in relation to their vision. The third day was focused on action planning and leadership: how were community members going to work together to bridge the gap between their current reality and their vision, and who in the village was going to lead the various practical initiatives they conceived? Villagers initially attended these workshops expecting to get the usual handout, but they never did. URDT stuck to its belief that the organization could only "teach people to fish." That is, leaders persisted with the idea that "no one can develop you until you make the choice to develop yourself."

Most of the villagers in Kibaale district were deeply enmeshed in the "poverty trap." They lived hand to mouth—and because they had very poor nutrition and bad water, they were unhealthy. This meant they had very little energy to take initiatives for improving their lives. This made them even more reactive, and stuck in a hand-to-mouth existence. "We would drink unboiled water. The children used to become sick with stomach diseases. I had an interest in my grandchildren going to school, but I was disadvantaged and didn't know how I would afford school fees or requirements [uniforms, school supplies]," Aidah recalled.

Felicita described how it felt for her: "I had no vision. I would just study. I never thought about where I would get money. I never imagined I would go to secondary school because our income was low."

URDT worked with this reality by helping the Nabasita family, and many others like them, focus on what would give them more energy (such as clean water and better nutrition). They also helped the villagers get energized by giving them a systems view of their circumstances, and a positive view of the resources they did have to create new visions for their families and their community.

After learning a new systemic perspective, villagers determined the basic actions that they needed to take to be healthy and begin pulling out of the poverty trap. For example, they had always been told by health workers, "you must boil water," but they often did not. When the villagers investigated the situation systemically, they gained insights into why this very significant, and seemingly simple, act was so difficult for them to perform. Boiling water as a routine practice required the right pots, fuel for boiling, skills and knowledge regarding boiling, a proper fireplace, containers to keep the boiled water clean, and money to buy or make the pot and containers. With the guidance of URDT, other basic interventions selected by villagers included spring protection, well digging, vegetable growing, and new sanitation practices.

From here, URDT worked with villagers to go further: What did they want for their lives beyond better living conditions? They engaged villagers to build roads from their villages into Kagadi Town—a town whose planning and organizing URDT had participated in alongside the local government so that it would become the "boomtown" it is today. As URDT writes on its Web site, "In 1999, Kagadi sub-county was estimated to have a population of 3,000. In 2004, the best estimate was over 25,000 residents. URDT training of local people has opened opportunities for many new businesses, often financed by local Savings and Credit Societies that URDT helped get started, and continues to support. Hundreds of new shops have opened, and many new small business buildings are under construction. Confidence in the future is demonstrated everywhere."

URDT started to build its own organic demonstration plots, and eventually an 80-acre organic farm, to show farmers how to develop their land better and grow cash crops. URDT staff have worked out the cost-benefit and breakeven points on every crop; they teach local farmers how to use small plots to maximize yields while working within the environmental constraints they face.

The district was rife with disputes over land ownership and the villagers wanted peace. In response, URDT established the land rights desk to facilitate peaceful resolutions. The villagers wanted ways to earn a living that did not depend on land ownership: a vocational institute was created with a microfinance bank for graduates and small borrowers to get started on new business enterprises. Human rights became a focal point for villagers as they drew upon their new energy to stand up to injustices within families and villages. URDT's human rights desk and the URDT radio station KKCR—the first community station in eastern Africa (with 2 million listeners today)—were established to educate and sensitize villagers to human rights issues, and to resolve such issues between them. It is also the easiest way for villagers to access crucial learning on ways to improve their quality of life.

Aidah describes how these programs have affected villagers' lives saying, "We listen to KKCR for the education programs, agriculture programs, and the human rights program. Since coming to URDT, we have built a new house and improved the drying rack and toilets. The new house has a tin roof instead of thatch, and four rooms. Now we boil our water. The children are not falling sick as frequently."

The URDT Girls School established in 2000 is a direct effort to address an economic development barrier created by a gender-based imbalance in opportunities in the community. As was the case in other districts of Uganda, girls and women were clearly the most underprivileged sector of Kibaale district—parents put their sons through school if they could afford school fees at all, and the quality of any girls' schools was very low. URDT could see that there were no options for orphaned and very poor girls to get an education. The award-winning URDT Girls School is a direct response to this. Alida Bakema-Boon joined the original cofounders to create the school, designing it with multiple purposes to fit their strategy of integrated rural development.

They challenged the myth that poor people don't have the same aspirations or capabilities as people with more means to create wealth for themselves and their children. They knew that parents, even when deep in the poverty trap, can be counted on to take pride in their children's accomplishments and hope for a better future for their children. Based on this assumption, the Girls School is developing female students as change agents who bring life and energy back into the family from their experience at school. By teaching their parents how to plan and implement projects at home, the girls are pulling their families out of poverty. At the same time, the gender inequalities for girls and women are being shifted; there is a more positive view of the value of a girl child in the home. Now girls like Felicita are seen as people who can create economic value instead being seen as a liability.

The creation of the African Rural University for Women (ARU) is the most recent facet of the URDT vision. With the success of the secondary school and many other thriving projects, in July 2003, the URDT board of directors recommended that a planning group begin serious work on making the ARU a reality. This will be the first rural university for women in Africa where young women will prepare to become entrepreneurs and leaders of rural development projects, using the creative orientation, visionary approach to planning, and other capabilities that have been developed through experience over the years. Graduates of the university will have the capacities to expand the impact of URDT, not only in Uganda but also in other African countries. This represents the model coming full circle in a sustainable cycle of growth. The beneficiaries of URDT's approach will teach others to help themselves, building a sustainable cycle of growth and opportunity for poor rural communities.

EXAMPLES OF URDT'S FLOURISHING RANGE OF INITIATIVES

The following are illustrations of the breadth and depth of the programs and initiatives that have been developed over time in response to needs and aspirations of people in the district, following the URDT model of integrated rural development.

Community Services	Education	Development Ventures
KKC Radio – 1st community development radio in East Africa	**URDT Girls School**	Community organizing of cooperative groups
Demonstration organic farm	Award winning	Collaborations with schools, government and NGOs
Library and resource centre	Residential for 210 bright, poor girls	Water protection and reserves for dry season
Business services – computer and internet training	Two generations education – children and parents	Farming methods
Human rights and land rights advocacy and mediation	"Back home" projects to raise family's standard of living	Maize milling
	URDT Vocational Institute	Fish farming
	For rural youth	Beekeeping
	Business, media and vocational studies	Construction and road building
	Leadership, entrepreneurship	Microfinance
	URDT Center for Reflection and Development	Solar energy and appropriate technology
	Capacity building for NGOs	Mechanic services
	Hands-on learning for development	Wood and metal work
	African Rural University for Women	Environmental conservation
	Under development now	
	Capacity building to replicate URDT story	
	Focus on visionary leadership, rural development, gender, entrepreneurship and technology	

Principles for Success

URDT is now, after 17 years, able to say unequivocally that it has created sustainable rural development in the district of Kibaale. The impact of this work is also emerging in neighboring districts. Top leaders in the country have taken notice of URDT, including Uganda's president, Yoweri Museveni, and have come to URDT to learn from its model. The leaders of URDT have developed principles for their work that have put long-term development efforts on solid footing, when prior conditions seemed hopeless. Where people formerly felt paralyzed because they perceived they had nothing but themselves, URDT has taught the local people to understand that they are the key to their own development. URDT has taught them how to create entirely different positive futures. URDT has proved to outsiders that there is another way besides handouts, aid, missionary work, or any other form of specialized "help." Instead, URDT has held to the following principles, which are applicable beyond Uganda and in situations even more disadvantaged than Kibaale district. We believe these principles to be the bedrock of any sustainable development strategy.

The premises that inform URDT's strategies and programs are, in the NGO's own words:

URDT's Development philosophy: *Lasting change is possible when people shift from reacting to circumstance to being creators of their own desired circumstances.*

URDT's Approach: Integrated and holistic. The household is integrated in its operations. It is imperative for any intervention to build on this old tested arrangement.

1. The people of Uganda, like all people the world over, are key to their own development—"no-one can develop you until you make the choice."
2. Lasting change is possible when people shift to the creative rather than the reactive orientation.
3. A people with a common vision can transcend traditional prejudices caused by tribal, religious, political, gender, and age differences and work together to achieve what is most important for them.
4. People have innate power and wisdom which they can tap to transform the quality of their life and that of their communities.
5. The training, education, and information sharing are key critical ingredients for rural transformation.

These principles are actively used in the continuous transfer of ideas to villages and households. In our view and from our direct experience visiting and interviewing key players at URDT and within Kibaale district, we also see a deeper set of foundational principles that underpin the URDT success. These guide all their actions and specific initiatives at an individual, household, village, and district level.

1. When working from a creative orientation, ensure that the vision, not current reality, is dominant. This is a fundamentally different orientation than that of problem solving.

2. Anchor the vision in individual commitment to take practical actions, rather than in theory and concepts. The vision must come from the people affected. If the vision comes from the intervenors, its impact will be low; it will be similar to receiving another handout or imposed idea. Since the poverty trap (and creativity deficit) is a huge barrier, action must come from what the people who aspire to change can truly imagine and manage, especially in the early stages of a shift.

3. Teach people how to "fish in the pond they have chosen," and build in the expectation they will then teach others how to fish, to contribute to the cycle (for example, girl students learn, then teach parents and other members of their community).

4. Help people see (make visible) and challenge (inquire into) disabling mental models such as the tendency to think in the collective negative (the "disempowered we"), which arises when people believe that power lies somewhere else—in God, luck, or the government, for example. When the "disempowered we" is in power, people cannot build on the idea that a personal vision is within their grasp.

5. Be honest and thorough about the assessment of current reality, both positive and negative aspects. Build a collective commitment to the truth above all else, and connect it to a vision of hope and progress. Insist on integrity, honesty, and transparency, and use this commitment to confront corruption and dishonesty wherever it

might appear. At the URDT school, the girls are vigilant in upholding this principle.

6. Help people see the linkages between issues (water pot, fuel, storage containers) so that they can take actions in the right order to achieve their vision (drink clean water). This is the core of the integrated development model at URDT.

7. Leverage the power of place. This makes it possible to ask, "What is it time for now, here, in this village?" Working within a specific village and district makes the power of systemic thinking come alive. This means visions are developed within the organizing principle of a whole life and a whole community, where a long-term orientation naturally arises.

Conclusions

URDT has accomplished all these outcomes in an integrated way; it has made progress on the U.N.'s Millennium Development Goals. Seventeen years ago, when URDT began its work, there were no millennium goals. Citizens of Kibaale did not require the U.N. to tell them what they wanted for their lives—with URDT's help, they have come to articulate very well what they want. As they made progress on their initial goals, other goals emerged. In a way, each goal, when met, led them to their next goal.

Those living in the developed world and working for corporations may read this story and think of it as simply a good example of how development in a poor country should occur. But maybe it is much more than that. Perhaps it is an archetypal story that contains lessons about how change can occur and what impedes those of us who work in the for-profit, developed world. Perhaps our companies also act like the U.N. tends to, dispensing directives with single points of resolution to isolated problems. For example, in terms of sustainability, how often do we approach it solely by addressing recycling or energy conservation in the office? Is this not a rather narrow approach to what is undoubtedly a systemic and pervasive set of challenges to us? In some corporate settings, "green" is understood to be the new politically correct way to manage. Perhaps only when employees and their leaders realize that sustainability for their company means sustainability for their region, city, and household will they become more effective in creating substantive strategies that are beyond "greenwashing."

Questions to Consider:

Reflect on the URDT story in relation to yourself and the world you live in:

If URDT can move toward sustainability in Kibale District, where people have virtually nothing, what does it mean for sustainability where you live and work?

How does the current abundance of wealth in our Western world impede real progress?

Can URDT's model, principles, and approach guide long-term change for us? How?

If we assume all the lessons and principles of change as developed by URDT do apply more broadly, what insights does that provoke?

What do you think would happen in a corporate or organizational setting if, in the process of trying to create change, leaders thought of themselves first as members of a community, rather than defining themselves by their roles in the professional setting?

Will we make sustainable progress if we assume we can impose a vision on others?

Resources

Uganda Rural Development and Training Programme: www.urdt.net

The United Nations Millenium Project; The U.N. Millenium Goals: www.un.org/millenniumgoals

10

Nike's Internal Environmental Activist

Ann Graham

Since Sarah Severn joined Nike in 1993, she has been among a group of employees who have made their careers a platform for advocating, investigating, and instigating sustainability policies and strategies at Nike, and for pressing their ideas into the competitive global sports footwear, apparel, and equipment industry. Severn says one reason she chose to work for a large multinational is that she believes in the power of global companies such as Nike to influence the attitudes and actions of other companies and consumers.

As one of the first professionals at Nike to bring the social and environmental perspective front and center in the business, Severn has witnessed and participated in significant change in the last 13 years, including the company's and the industry's turnaround performance in improving the human welfare of workers in foreign factories through the development of global standards for fair labor practices.

She began her Nike career in the marketing department, then held several pathbreaking environmental and social strategy positions that helped focus top management's attention on the importance of performance in these areas. In her current area, which is called "Horizons," she is charged with scanning the world for leading indicators of trends and new ideas that affect Nike's business and its efficacy as an agent for positive social

and environmental change in the world. Severn is currently part of a cor-
porate responsibility (CR) team of close to 100 people who are taking Nike's
decade-plus experience with sustainability strategy to the next level.

I did not end up working for Corporate America intentionally. I started my career as a consultant in market research and advertising in
London. During the 1980s, I was a strategic account planner, which
in essence meant using consumer insights to create strategy for advertising campaigns. When I joined Nike in 1993, I moved to the
Netherlands and started their European Consumer Insights group.

That's how I found myself involved in sustainability work. With a
degree in psychology, I have always been fascinated by consumer
behavior. What is the motivation behind our consumer choices? Can a
company that is environmentally responsible actually inspire a consumer to buy its product for that reason?

In the late 1980s in the U.K., there was a growing movement toward
buying green. Then we hit a recession, and green products were seen as
a luxury. People's interest in environmental issues seemed to peter
out—they were back in survival mode. It wasn't until things began to
improve economically in the mid-1990s that the green consumer started to reemerge.

Surveys of European consumers at that time showed them moving
away from a hedonistic phase to more of a values-based way of being.
This sort of shift in values ultimately shows up in people's consuming
behavior. Not everybody was changing consumption habits, but that's
where the leading edge of society was going. Nike Environmental
Action Team (NEAT), a very small group of people interested in examining environmental issues, formed in 1993. I was asked to do some
work for them and then, ultimately, to join the team. When the U.S.
director moved into another position within Nike, I moved to the U.S.
and stepped in to head NEAT. Initially NEAT had been focused on
developing innovative programs in areas such as waste management
and regulatory compliance, but until 1995, we had no overall perspective on sustainability. Once I took over the director role, we were heavily influenced by Paul Hawken's treatise in *The Ecology of Commerce*,

the Natural Step framework, and ultimately Bill McDonough's views on cradle-to-cradle design and product innovation.

When the focus turned in the mid-1990s to overseas manufacturing issues in contract factories where Nike products are made (we called it "the labor issue"), it took us by surprise. Nike's initial response was very defensive. This time was a real learning exercise for us: We finally realized the best way to meet that type of criticism was to find out what was happening, and to work on remedies. Now we take responsibility for how the people who work for our subcontractors and make our products are treated.

Over time we have also come to realize that we need to collaborate across the industry, to effect systemic change, through our code of conduct, auditing, and remediation mechanisms. Many of our subcontractors work with multiple brands, and they have to undergo multiple audits against a diverse array of codes. There are areas of our business where we have to be fiercely competitive, but labor practices is not one of those areas. One company on its own cannot tackle the big, global, systemic issues, like climate change and factory conditions. You have to partner with people and come to solutions together.

Today we have approximately 100 people in our CR group based in our world headquarters and in the regions, and they are aligned with the functions of our business. There are people in our group doing strategic planning, watching the risks and opportunities on the horizon (which is my role), working on product development, focusing on community investment as well as labor and environment, and ensuring health and safety compliance. We work with business leads in strategic planning, design and development, sourcing, global branding, and our regional leadership with the goal of integrating corporate responsibility and sustainability into the heart of our business.

Since 2002, I have been focused on corporate reporting and stakeholder engagement. My group had responsibility for a program called "Reuse-A-Shoe," which takes back defective returns and post-consumer shoes. In the U.S., for example, we work with the National Recycling Coalition, and together we set up collection sites throughout the United States. Consumers can bring worn-out shoes there and we take them back and process them. The materials are then licensed to companies that make sports surfaces, such as basketball courts, running tracks, playgrounds, football fields, and soccer fields. The program has been so successful that it is being expanded to other parts of the world.

As a brand we have incredible power to take a leadership role in sustainability. These and other initiatives are tangible examples of how the whole notion of sustainability, and of life thriving, both tie in with Nike's mission. We believe in the power of sports and physical activity to do enormously beneficial things for all people. As part of our mission statement we reference a quote from Nike cofounder Bill Bowerman: "If you have a body, you are an athlete." Sports bring people joy, health and fitness, and opportunity. Sports are very much about enhancing life.

It has taken time for our corporate culture to embrace sustainability and to recognize it as part of our mission. We have changed a lot in the last few years. In 1999 we tried a sustainability change initiative. It was a nine-month intensive learning program for Nike employees across departments about what it means to be a sustainable company. The idea was to create agents of change within Nike who would educate others, and help transform the company.

But the company wasn't entirely ready. It was before senior management really understood and embraced the idea of sustainability. Such an effort two or three years later would have had more traction. The difference now is not only that sustainability has become part of our core values, but that we have a framework where we have very clear corporate goals for our responsibilities in the world: to effect systemic change in working conditions in the footwear and apparel industry, to invest in design and innovation to create sustainable products, and to create access to sports and physical activity as a right for young people. There's a point at which you have to let people find out for themselves what they think works for the business and what doesn't. You cannot thrust things down anyone's throat. For me, and my colleagues at Nike who are at the forefront of defining sustainability strategy, that means if people in the business unit want to do things in a certain way—

which may not be exactly the vision we have—we need to let them, or come back to it with a different angle.

I have changed, too. Four years ago, when I was in my mid-40s, I went to Ecuador with John Perkins [author of *Confessions of an Economic Hit Man*], who was then the director of a group called Dream Change. We visited the Shuar, an indigenous group that used to be headhunters. There's a saying: "The world is as you dream it." In America we have dreamed a way of life that is destructive and rapacious. We build big buildings and we drive gas-guzzling cars. That's our reality. The Shuar beliefs are very different, as is their dream. They want to live as close to the Earth as possible, as part of a complete system. It was a transformative experience. It was the first time I had ever been in the Amazon rain forest. It is so alive. You hear animals calling to each other and the sounds of the forest, even at night. That trip reinforced my belief that the work I do is the right work. It also made me less afraid of being open about how I feel on these issues. I think probably for the first time, I really understood what we risk losing.

Inspired by a story by Joe Jaworski, one of the authors of *Presence*, I took a Sacred Passage trip in February 2006 to Baja with John Milton, a noted ecologist and spiritual teacher who leads guided passages into wilderness areas around the globe.

This group passage included a six-night solo camping experience next to the ocean, during the gray whale migration to their northern summer feeding grounds. Nature became my teacher and reminded me profoundly of the connections between species, and the need to reframe and transform our perception of humans' relationship with nature. We are operating under the illusion of "power over nature" when really it is "one with nature."

Resources

www.sacredpassage.com

www.naturalstep.org

John Perkins, *Confessions of an Economic Hit Man*, Berrett-Kohler, 2004

11

Reebok's Human Rights
Standard-Bearer

Ann Graham

Since 1992, Reebok International Ltd. has implemented a voluntary fair labor standards code of conduct—the Reebok Human Rights Production Standards—in the independently owned and operated factories that manufacture its products. Doug Cahn, who joined Reebok in 1991 following a stint working on public policy issues in Washington D.C., was appointed to lead Reebok's Human Rights programs in 1991. The Canton, Massachusetts-based company was the first athletic footwear company to develop a code of conduct for subcontractor factories. Doug Cahn drafted that document. At the time, the poor treatment of overseas workers by foreign multinationals was just beginning to make headlines in the Western media. Today, as a Reebok vice president, Cahn supervises a human rights field team of 20 people, who mostly live in the countries of production in South and East Asia. This team is dedicated to educating factories and trading agents (about Reebok's standards and helping to apply those standards. Cahn also directs the human rights grant making for the Reebok Human Rights Foundation and leads an annual award program to honor young human rights activists.

Before I came to Reebok, I was involved in human rights and foreign policy issues in Washington, D.C. I worked for three Democrats in the House of Representatives over 13 years. I left Capitol Hill because my wife got a job in Boston. I didn't know what I would end up doing. I considered standard-fare corporate jobs, working for a real estate developer or a bank, but these jobs did not interest me. I looked for many months before I got a call from Sharon Cohen; she was at the time a vice president of public affairs at Reebok, and was developing the company's human rights positioning and processes. She asked me to direct the Reebok Human Rights program. At that time I knew very little about the footwear business.

Back in 1988, on the 40th anniversary of the signing of the United Nations' Universal Declaration of Human Rights, Amnesty International USA created a 26-city concert tour featuring top rock stars—Bruce Springsteen, Sting, Peter Gabriel, and many other high-profile performers. They needed corporate underwriting for what would become known as the Human Rights Now! Concert Tour. Reebok was red-hot in the marketplace but had no corporate giving program. The board of directors and our chairman, Paul Fireman, decided to invest $10 million in the tour. Human rights was a global issue, and as a global brand we realized we were in a position to take a stand. Plus, there were important reasons for us to do this as a business. It was gratifying when employees who worked on the tour came back inspired to do more. Reebok created an awards ceremony to honor young activists working nonviolently on an issue related to human rights. We have been giving an annual award since then; 80 people from 35 countries have been recipients.

During my first months at Reebok, it became clear that we needed to look beyond brand positioning to examine our own business practices. The Human Rights program included many young, vocal activists. They pushed us to consider our obligation to the laborers making our shoes. Employees asked questions, too. I remember talking to other Reebok employees in late 1991. These were their questions: "Well, what are we doing in our supply chain?" "Have we talked to our suppliers about the conditions of labor in the factories that our partners run?"

The senior management at Reebok was receptive to establishing a code of conduct for the subcontracted factories where Reebok shoes were being made. They essentially told me, "Go make it happen." So I did. I convened a task force that included our general counsel, the heads of our supply chains for footwear and for apparel, and our CFO. We met several times in late 1991 and early 1992, consulting with an attorney, Diane Orentlicher, who had been active in the human rights world. She was an expert on the International Labour Organization (ILO) standards. She helped us understand how we could benchmark against ILO labor standards create our own corporate code.

Diane came to headquarters and we spent a half-day laying out the project in a way we thought would be useful for the task force. Then I spent considerable time asking questions. It was tricky. I remember ad hoc conversations with our general counsel, who had a particular set of concerns about words that would impact risk and liability, and would have to be broadly applied through our supply chain. When this work was done and the CEO, Paul Fireman, came to a meeting, he asked whether the code of conduct we had drafted represented the consensus of the working group. We said, "Yes." Paul said, "This code of conduct is approved." It was a very short meeting.

The code itself was accompanied by an implementation plan. We had to present the standards at the annual convention of our footwear suppliers. I flew to Bali, Indonesia, to make that presentation. Then the process of inspection and assessment began. We asked the factory managers to fill out a questionnaire to give us their view of operations relative to the new standards we had set. I remember getting a call one morning, very late in the evening Hong Kong time, from Reebok's vice president of production. "Doug," he said, "I've looked through all the completed audit forms from the factories. I don't think they understand what we're asking them to do. You need to come assess conditions in these factories yourself."

In hindsight, it seems obvious that was what we should have done in the first place. At the time, though, to create an internal monitoring function to assess workplace conditions in factories halfway around the world was a major initiative. We knew it was time-consuming and required leadership. In fact, it took three of us: our internal auditor, Ed Tutless, whose job it was to audit a range of issues within the company; Henry Ching, the general manager of Reebok's business office in Hong Kong, who knew the factories and had relationships with the owners; and me, because I knew the standards. Together, we set off to audit all of the footwear factories in Asia on a grueling three-week trip.

The first footwear factory I ever went into was in Indonesia. I had never seen such a large industrial plant. There were thousands and thousands of workers. Line after line, all dutifully performing a particular function, at the end of which were beautiful, clean, well-designed, well-manufactured Reebok shoes in boxes ready for shipment. I remember spending that day not actually assessing the workplace, but sitting in the boardroom trying to figure out what to do. How do you logically and systematically make judgments about the conditions in this factory? How do you know what's good and what's bad? It was clear that this was not a factory with child laborers. There were odors in the factory. But I kept thinking, How did we know if they were toxic? How were we to understand the complex pay system to determine whether wages were appropriate?

I came away from that experience with many more questions than answers, but I also learned it was better to evaluate a few things than to do a sweeping assessment. As time went on, our ability to understand conditions—both my personal ability and our team's—became more sophisticated. We learned more about local law, about air quality, and the threshold limits for solvents. We hired an industrial hygienist who trained us to analyze the environmental impact of these chemicals. We picked a few core issues and boiled down a 40-page questionnaire about the conditions in the factory to two sides of a little cardboard poster. We kept a copy of that poster in our back pockets when we walked around the factory. On one side there was a series of specific health- and safety-related checks; on the other were questions related to working hours and wages. For example, there are huge, hot drums that are rolled to press the rubber into sheets. These drums didn't have any safety mechanism on them. So if a hand or a limb were to get caught in a drum, there was no way to stop it from rolling. Today, there are safety bars on the drums and you can hit a button to stop it. The bars are there because we told the factories they had to have them.

Our approach to improving standards is not punitive, though. When we see problems, we rarely terminate relationships. Instead, we try to get the factory up to speed. Still, experience has also given us an appreciation of what it takes for a factory to implement our standards. We now have a more comprehensive range of compliance benchmarks. We are better at identifying potential problems that could be related to a particular code provision. And we communicate those requirements to factories and audit against them. This year we will print our fourth edition of the guide explaining our code. It's a much fatter guidebook than it was when we started. This guidebook goes to the factories, trading agencies, our own internal sourcing, and production managers. It is on our Web site so anybody can access it.

We don't want to be the police anymore—going in, finding problems, confronting management, and insisting on deadlines. Management has to be able to demonstrate that they have systems in place to communicate with their workforce, that workers who are having problems can address them with management, free of fear and intimidation. We want to know that the code of conduct is being applied honestly, and not just on a day when we show up to do an assessment.

In many of the subcontractor factories, our product is on a line next to a competitor's products, but labor standards is not an area where we compete. Our competitors come to us on a regular basis to ask specific questions about a factory where we both produce goods. We routinely meet with companies in the apparel and footwear industry to talk to them about our successes, our failures, future initiatives, and how we can all help to do more.

In the early years of this work, the major footwear companies did not collaborate. Now, Adidas, Nike, Puma, and Reebok all participate in the Fair Labor Association (FLA). The FLA is a multi-stakeholder initiative—an organization that is governed not only by business, but also by consumer groups, universities, labor groups, and human rights organizations. Companies that participate must agree to a set of obligations, including independent monitoring of 5 percent of a company's factories each year.

In 2004 I talked with Peter Burrows, our chief technology officer, about what it would take to get more companies in our industry involved. We decided to donate a million-dollar piece of software to the Fair Factories Clearinghouse. The software, called the Human Rights Tracking System, was developed to track information about workplace conditions in the factories. The Fair Factories Clearinghouse works in collaboration with two trade associations (the National Retail Federation and the Retail Council of Canada) and World Monitors Inc., a New York–based consulting firm that advises multinational companies on their labor standards.

With a common technology platform, we can share information with another company by pushing a button, instead of having ad hoc conversations. Technology is a nice convenience, but what is really important is that we all understand that no one company can succeed by doing this work alone.

Resources

Fair Factories Clearinghouse: www.fairfactories.org
Fair Labor Association: www.fairlabor.org
World Monitors, Inc.: www.worldmonitors.com

12

Sustainability: The Inner and Outer Work

Sara Schley

Over the years, many people devoted to sustainability have used the phrase "the triple bottom line" to articulate strategy. They don't focus solely on economic bottom-line activities: profitability, financial performance, or even the capacity to make a living. Instead, they judge success according to social and environmental results as well: by their ability to improve the natural environment and make people's lives better in society as a whole. The "triple bottom line" concept represented a great improvement over the constraints of a purely financial point of view, in which environmental and social results (including such business needs as customer satisfaction) were perceived as costs or externalities.

But ultimately, the triple bottom line is not sufficient. Initiatives based solely on this concept as a rationale—for example, efforts to change a company so that it can consistently produce "triple-bottom-line results"—often seem to falter. Moreover, the focus on the triple bottom line may draw people away from the qualities and attitudes they need if they are to genuinely make a difference in developing sustainable organizations, practices, and communities.

There seem to be two reasons for this. First, the way that most people operate with the triple bottom line ignores the real synergy among its three dimensions—social, economic, and ecological. In practice, efforts tend to be fragmented: Companies institute "social policies," "green practices," and financial reporting systems without ever linking them together. By contrast, projects with deep linkages can be powerfully effective. One example is the initiative by Dr. Macharia Waruingi to eradicate malaria in his home country of Kenya. This project connects investment in local businesses (which builds economic infrastructure), with the development of business capacity to make and sell mosquito repellent and bug nets, the reduction of environmental toxins, and the creation of local community support.

The second reason that a focus on the triple bottom line alone isn't enough is that it allows people to ignore the "inner work"—the personal practices and disciplines that provide the perspective and internal stability needed to make a difference in the long run. The very ideals and aspirations that lead people to an interest in sustainability can also drive people into a frenzied cycle of "fixes," actions, and imperatives, ultimately leading to wasted efforts and burned-out people. For our own sake, and that of the results we hope to produce, we need to prevent this from happening.

The answer lies in the inner work of sustainability. A reinforcing process is set in motion when people start to deliberately slow down their lives to cultivate broader awareness and reflective practice. The cycle, if we were to map it in systems thinking terms, would look something like this:

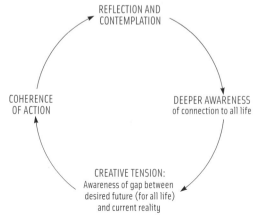

Deeper Awareness of the Connection to All Life

In college physics, years ago, I learned that the equation for gravitational attraction on the planetary scale is virtually the same as the equation for gravitational attraction on the atomic scale. In other words, "as above, so below." The structures at the largest astronomical scale are echoed in the structures of our cells. These correspondences are not obvious to the naked eye, and they may not be predictable, but they are far more powerful than people often expect.

Awareness of the underlying interconnectedness of life, wherever it started for you, may well lead you to feel a greater sense of responsibility for the whole. At heart, this represents a shift in mental models. You and I may start to see that our lives are interconnected with the lives of all living entities on earth, from microorganisms to all people to the ecosystem of the planet as a whole. We may gain a humble awareness that the small choices we make, day by day—what to consume, how to handle our garbage and waste, how to conduct our work, and how to spend our time—do indeed have effects on the larger systems around us. We may also start to recognize that our ability to care about others—people on far-flung continents, people in unfortunate circumstances, people caught in disasters, or people anywhere in the chain of life—makes a difference. We have creative and destructive capacity: We can act to contribute to life, healing, and generativity, or we can act with violence and fragmentation. When writer Janine Benyus said, "We have to fall back in love with nature," she was speaking in part about the importance of embracing this sense of interdependence. In my view, it makes an enormous difference to anyone's perspective and capabilities when they not only intellectually see interconnection, but emotionally feel it.

Creative Tension

Awareness of our connection to all things is a kind of vision; it leads us to wish for a better quality of life and equity for all people on the planet. At the same time, as this sense of connection to others increases, we become more aware of the suffering and problems that exist around us. Despite the success we may experience in our own individual professional and private lives, we come to recognize more coherently the gap between the world as it is and the world as it could be.

Stronger awareness of the gap, in turn, leads to one of two responses. First, as Joanna Macy and Dana Meadows have noted, it leads to denial and despair: People often throw up their hands and retreat into a shell. But confined spaces are boring, and sooner or later many of us emerge, aware of the gap that needs to be closed and interested in learning how to do our part to close it.

We may have an increased desire to take coherent action to bridge the gap for others, and for life in general. People who feel this desire are then more likely to take action "in service of life," with a more intensive desire to improve the economic, cultural, social and environmental well-being of all. In the process, people learn, bit by bit, to live with emotional tension, that is, to tolerate the fact that the gap between vision and current reality exists. And then we allow a different kind of tension in ourselves, the natural movement to close the gap, to come to the surface.

Coherence of Actions

Creative tension leads to better results. If we are attuned to the gap between vision and current reality, we pay more attention to the signals that come back to us in response to our actions. Either our actions have produced the results we want, and moved us closer to our aspirations, or they haven't. And if they haven't, we will pick up those signals and our actions will become more effective and coherent.

As people's capability and awareness grow, they choose to do better things—things naturally more in line with the aspirations of an integrated triple bottom line. These actions are inevitably more diverse than the habitual behaviors of people acting primarily in terms of their own self-interest. More coherent actions produce a wider variety of feedback—responses from the world—which naturally leads people to want to make sense of those responses, in the mind, body, and heart. This increases the value of the contemplative state.

Personal Contemplative Practice

Most of the successful people I know in the sustainability field regularly follow some discipline of contemplative practice. In workshops on sustainability, my colleagues and I often ask, "How many people set time aside for reflection or contemplation in some disciplined way?" Lately, nearly every hand goes up.

Like the individuals who practice them, forms of contemplation vary dramatically. People might practice prayer, meditation, yoga; walking in the woods, running on a track, or, in the case of one CEO we know, beekeeping. But all such practices have this in common: They quiet the mind, decrease the static in our systems, and allow us to put the treadmill of everyday life on hold. They sharpen our ability to see current reality, and act in accordance with our aspirations for self, family, community, and world.

Midwife and Buddhist teacher Terri Nash says that actions that are not grounded in contemplation do violence; to the extent they are grounded in some form of reflective practice, they become more coherent. The reverse is also true. As actions become more grounded and coherent, the quality of contemplative practice goes up.

In turn, as personal consciousness (developed through whatever reflective discipline is chosen) increases, a person's innate awareness of the connection to all life increases. Anyone who has practiced contemplative work recognizes this. And thus the reinforcing cycle is closed.

Contemplation is a critical part of the cycle, not just because of the mental process of reflection, but because of the cessation of the normal cycle of activity and consumption. One common practice, observing the Sabbath or Shabbat, is taking a day of rest, but not just from work: from other everyday activities such as shopping, talking on the telephone, and using e-mail. I know people who practice this faithfully from Friday evening to Saturday evening every week. That day is spent in awareness of the perfection of creation. No one buys anything because nothing is needed. No one talks on the phone or travels because perfection exists where we are, and with whoever is nearby. There is no television, Internet, or other media. The day is spent taking walks in the woods, exercising, meditating, connecting with family members and friends, dancing, conversing, laughing, and sharing meals. It adds up to a taste of the world to come. The boundaries set around that day make it a day of tremendous freedom.

And observing Sabbath or Shabbat influences habits for the rest of the week as well. On Sunday morning, the reasons for anxiety and stress, so overwhelming on Friday, are difficult to remember. The impetus to make needless purchases is gone. That in turn makes it easier, during the rest of the week, to resist otherwise addictive drives to push, grow, and consume.

The Role of Emotions

My colleagues and I have noticed that, for many people, the journey to sustainability begins with emotion. We may hear a report that 30,000 children will die of starvation after a natural disaster has occurred. There may be reason to believe that global climate change is involved in triggering the disaster. And we feel not just a sense of connection, but grief (mourning the loss), anger ("How was this allowed to happen?") or fear ("Could this happen again?") We may also feel the sense of joy that naturally arises when people are connected to each other and to the natural environment. For a variety of reasons, although we may have ignored these emotions in the past, we find them compelling us now.

The reader of this book may be used to thinking of emotions as destructive. Emotions can emerge in destructive ways. But emotions can also be expressed in constructive ways. Primary emotions have evolved in the human species over millennia. Anger and fear are hardwired in our biological systems, as are grief and joy. When we disown these emotions, we deny ourselves vital information that can be used to stay alive and achieve our aspirations. In many situations, emotions can be valuable as a kind of barometer—an indicator that there is something we need to reflect upon and figure out if we want our actions to be effective.

Emotions also play a critical role in organizational life. There is always a temptation to view businesses in an industrial-age way, as machines with people operating in the cogs; in such a view it seems appropriate to devalue emotions. What machine feels? Corporate cultures have developed a stoic resistance to emotions: People are supposed to "suck it up" and not express anger or fear. The mental model is that emotions make it harder to get work done. But not only is that a mistake, it's not possible. We are basically emotional beings. When a colleague says "I'm not angry! I'm just determined," stay tuned. As that individual tries to suppress his or her emotions, they will leak out in other ways.

Once you start to experience corporations and organizations as living systems, populated with living people, you then see that emotions are already playing an integral role in any serious sustainability effort there. Making emotions more explicit can have value. Without making our grief explicit, how can we find the motivation to get involved in efforts to save the 30,000 children who will otherwise die of starvation? Without exploring the anger we feel at the injustice of thousands of infants being born with mercury toxicity, how can we act to change that outcome in our industries and our regulations? Without naming our fear of the consequences of polar ice caps melting, how can we take the actions necessary to create clean and renewable energy sources? And without taking the time to draw forth the joy we feel in celebrating our achievements, how can we have the strength to endure? Emotions exist in all of us; they can provide an important source of initial energy and insight for any action-oriented learning process. It is time to reclaim them.

Emotions also give us feedback on the potential direction of our efforts—or those of our organization. For example, if anger is present, there is a good chance that there is some injustice in the system that needs to be addressed. If fear is present, there is a good chance that we need to raise our awareness of some imbalance in the system. If grief is present, we may have lost or be about to lose something precious. And if joy is present, there is a good chance we're on the right track. The trick is learning to distinguish the source of the anger, fear, grief, or joy. For example, is fear a justified signal of impending troubles, or an exaggerated personal fear reflected outward?

Our work is to increase our capacity to understand and interpret our emotional systems. The value of coaching often comes in helping people discern the many faces of grief, anger, joy, and fear and seeing what "wants" to happen—how do those emotions link to actions?

Suppose, for example, that you are outraged and angry about a report of those 30,000 children dying of starvation. Your emotions may lead you to open your heart and write a check to Oxfam or some other trustworthy agency. But what can you do, from the vantage point of your life's work, to make more of a difference—or to prevent such tragedies from occurring in the future?

It will take time and attention to design such an effort. A true commitment might mean leveraging your job; if you are an engineer at an oil company, that will take a certain form; if you are an editor at a nonprofit newsletter, a different form; a marketer at a consumer products firm, still another. It will mean defining your commitment: What is your vision for children? Is it simply to avoid starvation, or are you committed to doing what you can to provide life, food, caring guardians, and education? Since time and capabilities are limited, which children, in which contexts, in which ways, will you work to help? How much effort and time can you realistically put in without infringing on other commitments important to you? Will you be acting alone, or can you marshal the efforts of other people, either in an existing organization or in a group that coalesces for that purpose? Or is there an existing endeavor that you would do better to join?

You want a planet where your kids and all kids can thrive. As your vision for life grows, and as your awareness of current reality deepens, you may feel some despair at the vastness of the gap between the two. What can one person possibly do to make a difference? At the same time, you may also see a compelling need for new, more effective actions. As you increase your commitment to creating a planet where life thrives, you will find that a deepening understanding of your own emotional energy is essential, as is time for quiet reflection. And as your skill, intelligence, and heart for working in these domains grows, so does your capacity to be a wise, compassionate, and effective leader. These qualities will be reflected in the actions you take in service of sustainability, small and large, day to day.

ABOUT THE AUTHORS

Peter Senge

Peter Senge is a senior lecturer at the MIT Sloan School of Management, and the founding chair of SoL, the Society for Organizational Learning, a global network of learning communities addressing profound institutional change. SoL is an outgrowth of the former Center of Organizational Learning, founded and based at MIT, where Peter received his M.S. and Ph.D. A renowned pioneer in and writer about management innovation, Peter is the author of the widely acclaimed *The Fifth Discipline: The Art and Practice of the Learning Organization*. Peter lives with his wife and children in central Massachusetts.

Joe Laur

Joe Laur is founding partner with Sara Schley of Seed Systems, a company dedicated to promoting sustainable development in business and society through the use of organizational learning, systems thinking disciplines, and scientific conditions for sustainability. He has been working with whole systems change for 25 years. The former Executive Director of New Warrior Training Adventure, he received his B.F.A. from the University of Wisconsin and is certified by the Rolf Institute of Boulder, Colorado as a practitioner of Structural Integration. A naturalist and hunter, Joe lives in rural Massachusetts with his wife Sara Schley and their children.

Sara Schley

Sara Schley began her practice of organizational learning in the early 1990s with the Organizational Learning Center at MIT. She is co-steward and one of the original architects of the SoL Sustainability Consortium, a group of companies whose purpose is to create sustainable enterprises. With her partner Joe Laur, she runs the international consulting company Seed Systems. The author of numerous articles, Sara is the mother of four-year-old twins and lives in rural Massachusetts with Joe Laur and their children.

Bryan Smith

Bryan Smith is an internationally recognized author, speaker and consultant to business, education and government on leadership and innovation within the context of global sustainability. Prior to founding Broad Reach Innovations, Bryan was a senior partner for eighteen years at Innovation Associates, a firm that pioneered the field of Organizational Learning. He has been a central contributor to the development of the field and the creation of innovative tools and strategies for building inspired learning organizations. Bryan received his M.B.A. and Ph.D. in Organizational Behavior from the University of Toronto and lives in Toronto, Canada with his family.

ABOUT THE CONTRIBUTORS

Ann Graham is an independent journalist based in Edgartown, Massachusetts and Bronxville, New York. From 2000 to 2005 she was the Deputy Editor of *strategy+business* magazine, published by the management consulting firm, Booz Allen Hamilton. Prior to joining Booz Allen, Ann held senior editorial positions at Gartner, Inc., and *The Economist* and spent a decade as a country risk analyst for Merrill Lynch and several other economic research firms. She is the author of *Managing the Global Environmental Challenge: Strategies for Corporate Excellence* (Economist Intelligence Unit, New York, 1991). Her articles exploring the relationship between business strategy and societal welfare have appeared in numerous publications in Europe and the United States.

Chris Page is a member of Rocky Mountain Institute's Integrative Design Team and project leader for RMI's educational initiatives. For the past five years, she has co-facilitated various working groups for SoL's Sustainability Consortium, including the Materials Pooling project. She is part of a Ceres multistakeholder team advising a major restaurant chain on socially responsible business practices. An educator with over fifteen years' experience on three continents, she is currently developing a system dynamics computer model to help utilities manage carbon emissions. Chris is a Donella Meadows Leadership Fellow, a former NOLS instructor, and a member of Mountain Rescue Aspen, a volunteer search and rescue team.

Sue Simington is strategic consultant focused on corporate sustainability and value creation. Sue has held leadership roles at Levi Strauss & Company and at Sunnybrook Health Sciences Centre. For more than 15 years she has been an external consultant, working with clients in North America and Europe. Sue has designed and led forums for executive leaders, including chief negotiators of the Kyoto Protocol on Climate Change. Sue earned a Masters in Applied Behavioral Sciences after completing a degree in Business Administration at Queen's University. She lives with her family in Toronto, Canada.

Special thanks to Sharon Harkey, Art Kleiner, Nina Kruschwitz, Jennifer Margulis, and the members of the SoL Sustainability Consortium for their contributions and support in creating this book.

NOTES

1   United Nation's World Commission on Environment and Development, *Our Common Future*, Oxford University Press, 1987

2   John Ehrenfeld, "Searching for Sustainability: No Quick Fix," *Reflections: the SoL Journal*, Vol. 5 No. 8 (2004); www.solonline.org/reflections

3   William McDonough and Michael Braungart, *Cradle to Cradle*, North Point Press, 2002

4   Daniel Quinn, *Ishmael*, Bantam, 1991

5   Trend Micro, *Computer World*, January, 16, 2004; www.trendmicro.com

6   www.organicconsumers.org/btc/gasfood112105.cfm

7   The Alternative, *Sentaku*, Vol. 30, No. 5 (May 2004) pp. 122-125. Translated by Mieko Nishimizu.

8   Global sequestration is inherently difficult to measure, a problem exacerbated by the continuing deforestation and saturation of many "carbon sinks" by high present-day carbon concentration. The UNFCCC estimated global sequestration at about half the level of 2000 emissions, but *Scientific American* recently (September 2005) placed the "long-term rate of sustainable emissions" at less than one-quarter of the present rate.

9   www.m-dictionary/com/dictionary/sustainability

10 John Ehrenfeld, "Searching for Sustainability: No Quick Fix," *Reflections: the SoL Journal*, Vol. 5 No. 8 (2004); John Ehrenfeld, "The Roots of Sustainability," *Sloan Management Review*, Winter, 2005

11 William McDonough and Michael Braungart, *Cradle to Cradle*, North Point Press, 2002, p. 104

ABOUT SOL

SoL, The Society for Organizational Learning, is a nonprofit global membership organization that connects researchers, organizations, and consultants to create and implement knowledge for fundamental innovation and change. SoL members engage in a variety of forums, projects, and learning opportunities that expand their capacity for inspired performance and creating results together that could not be created alone.

As a self-organizing global learning community, SoL has a growing number of communities and consortia around the world organized by geography and focus. The purpose of the SoL Sustainability Consortium is to build the capacity in organizations and society to achieve economic, ecological and social sustainability. The Consortium actively practices the five disciplines of organizational learning and systems thinking in all it does, and engages leaders to work together across traditional boundaries to achieve shared aims. A list of current members and projects can be found at **www.solsustainability.org**.

SoL was founded in 1997 as an outgrowth of the MIT Center for Organizational Learning. The main office, located in Cambridge, MA, primarily supports the founding SoL community while also providing basic infrastructure for the global SoL community.

More information about projects, resources, communities, membership, and other publications can be found at **www.solonline.org**.